COMPLETE CONDITIONING FOR FOOTBALL

Pat Ivey

Josh Stoner

Human Kinetics

Library of Congress Cataloging-in-Publication Data

Ivey, Pat, 1972-
  Complete conditioning for football / Pat Ivey, Josh Stoner.
    p. cm.
  Includes index.
  ISBN-13: 978-0-7360-9319-4 (soft cover)
  ISBN-10: 0-7360-9319-2 (soft cover)
  1. Football--Training. I. Stoner, Josh, 1975- II. Title.
  GV953.5.I84 2012
  796.33207--dc23
                                2011033470

ISBN-10: 0-7360-9319-2 (print)
ISBN-13: 978-0-7360-9319-4 (print)

This publication is written and published to provide accurate and authoritative information relevant to the subject matter presented. It is published and sold with the understanding that the author and publisher are not engaged in rendering legal, medical, or other professional services by reason of their authorship or publication of this work. If medical or other expert assistance is required, the services of a competent professional person should be sought.

The web addresses cited in this text were current as of September 2011, unless otherwise noted.

Acquisitions Editor: Justin Klug; **Developmental Editor:** Cynthia McEntire; **Assistant Editor:** Elizabeth Evans; **Copyeditor:** Patsy Fortney; **Indexer:** Dan Connolly; **Graphic Designer:** Fred Starbird; **Graphic Artist:** Kim McFarland; **Cover Designer:** Keith Blomberg; **DVD Face Designer:** Susan Rothermel Allen; **DVD Producer:** Doug Fink; **Video Production Coordinator:** Amy Rose; **Photographer (cover):** Hunter Martin/Getty Images; **Photo Production Manager:** Jason Allen; **Art Manager:** Kelly Hendren; **Associate Art Manager:** Alan L. Wilborn; **Illustrations:** Tammy Page; **Printer:** McNaughton & Gunn

We thank the University of Missouri in Columbia, Missouri, for assistance in providing the location for the shoot for this book.

Human Kinetics books are available at special discounts for bulk purchase. Special editions or book excerpts can also be created to specification. For details, contact the Special Sales Manager at Human Kinetics.

The contents of this DVD are licensed for private home use and traditional, face-to-face classroom instruction only. For public performance licensing, please contact a sales representative at www.HumanKinetics.com/SalesRepresentatives.

Printed in the United States of America   10   9   8   7   6   5   4   3   2   1

The paper in this book is certified under a sustainable forestry program.

Human Kinetics
Website: www.HumanKinetics.com

United States: Human Kinetics
P.O. Box 5076
Champaign, IL 61825-5076
800-747-4457
e-mail: humank@hkusa.com

Canada: Human Kinetics
475 Devonshire Road Unit 100
Windsor, ON N8Y 2L5
800-465-7301 (in Canada only)
e-mail: info@hkcanada.com

Europe: Human Kinetics
107 Bradford Road
Stanningley
Leeds LS28 6AT, United Kingdom
+44 (0) 113 255 5665
e-mail: hk@hkeurope.com

Australia: Human Kinetics
57A Price Avenue
Lower Mitcham, South Australia 5062
08 8372 0999
e-mail: info@hkaustralia.com

New Zealand: Human Kinetics
P.O. Box 80
Torrens Park, South Australia 5062
0800 222 062
e-mail: info@hknewzealand.com

E5139

To my wife, Starla, that we continue to grow together on
our journey to being the best people we can be.
And to my daughters, Paisli and Serena, that you believe
you can accomplish anything you set your minds to.

Pat Ivey

To my wife, Christin, that we continue to
work to bring out the best in each other
and provide great role models for our children.
To my sons, Jarrett and Jackson, that you continue to
develop your sense of fun, respect, pride, and love
and develop the courage to accomplish your goals.

Josh Stoner

Contents

DVD Contents vi

Foreword by Gary R. Pinkel viii

Preface ix

Acknowledgments xi

PART I   PROGRAM FEATURES. . . .1

Chapter 1   Training Philosophy 3

Chapter 2   Testing and Evaluation 15

Chapter 3   Nutrition and Recovery. 41

PART II   EXERCISES 51

Chapter 4   Warm-Up and Flexibility 53

Chapter 5   Speed 69

Chapter 6   Quickness and Agility 89

Chapter 7 Power 103

Chapter 8 Strength 121

Chapter 9 Conditioning............. 177

PART III TRAINING SCHEDULE AND WORKOUTS.....187

Chapter 10 Off-Season Workouts 189

Chapter 11 Spring and Summer Workouts................ 213

Chapter 12 In-Season Workouts 237

Additional Resources 247

Index 248

About the Authors 252

DVD Contents

Warm-Up and Flexibility

Tapioca
Front Bear Crawl
Crab Walk
Stationary Dynamic Movements
    Arm Circles
    Trunk Rolls
    Knee Up and Across
    Knee Tuck
    Iliotibial (IT) Band

Speed

B-March/B-Skip
High Knee
Running Butt Kick
Fast Leg
Dead Leg
Bounding
40-Yard Stance and Start

Quickness and Agility

Mat Drills
    High Knees Mat Drill
    Two-Point Shuffle Wave Mat Drill
    Two-Point Seat Roll Mat Drill
    Four-Point Seat Roll Mat Drill
    Four-Point Directional Wave Mat Drill
    Two-Point Sprint Wave Mat Drill
    Mirror Mat Drill
    Spinning Wheel Mat Drill
    Quarter Eagle Mat Drill
Cone Drills
Speed Ladder Drills
Five-Cone Drills

Power

Broad Jump
Split Jump
Plyometric Push-Up
Medicine Ball Chest Pass
Hang Clean

Strength

Back Squat
Front Squat
Dead Lift
Strongman
Hurdles
Scap Circuit
Pistol Squat
Tate Press

Total Running Time . . . . **46 minutes**

Foreword

I am excited to support and recommend *Complete Conditioning for Football*. Strength and conditioning and athletic performance coaches play an integral role in the development of football players. In this book, Pat Ivey and Josh Stoner outline and deliver some of the best training techniques available to maximize athletic performance in football players.

Pat Ivey and Josh Stoner have worked together since 2002 and have brought their collective experience to the University of Missouri Tigers football team. Their influence has been invaluable in our success during our run of several bowl games and three Big 12 North championships. Pat and Josh bring their past experiences as both football players and coaches into this project. They bring educational backgrounds in exercise science and physiology, sport nutrition, business, education, and sports psychology to design a comprehensive, integrated approach to training. They understand how to train athletes to be prepared to be better football players at all levels.

In the ever-evolving field of athletic performance, it is important to stay current with the science, technology, and research, while combining that knowledge with the art of coaching. Today's players are bigger, faster, stronger, and more agile than ever and it takes a special understanding of how to train these athletes, which is where the art of coaching lives. First you have to care about your athletes as people and then you will get the results you desire.

Complete Conditioning for Football presents some of the latest and most innovative methods of training available to maximize your athletic performance. This book/DVD package will transform you and your training program and allow you to unlock your athletic potential by outlining a step-by-step process of progression. If you really want to dominate and be the best football athlete you can be, use the methods in this book and you will be on your way to delivering your best performances.

Gary R. Pinkel, Head Football Coach, University of Missouri

Preface

The Navy Seals have a saying: "The only easy day was yesterday." This is exactly the mindset needed for football players to train successfully and continue that success. This is the approach we have used during our year-round training process and the successes speak for themselves.

As you read through this book, you may recognize some of the concepts; some may not be as recognizable. The organization and knowledge contained in the following chapters are a culmination of many years of trial and error and the active seeking out of information from any and all sources that could help our program. We have read books, visited other training facilities, practiced what we have preached, and found ways to grow.

This book is designed to give you an idea of what we do in a general sense but it would be incorrect to assume that all the variables can be covered. Often there are constraints to the design and administration of athletic performance enhancement protocols, including time constraints, equipment challenges, time of season, availability, number of athletes on the team, number of staff available, and the experience level of that staff. It is a challenge, both for the athletic performance coach and the athlete, but it can be accomplished. You must be willing to learn and adapt at all times, both in your knowledge of athletic performance and the environment in which the athletes are trained.

Complete Conditioning for Football takes into consideration the variables necessary for creating a holistic approach to training, from developing a training philosophy all the way to effective recovery techniques. The core of what we do is to improve athletic performance and as such we must recognize that the same programming during the freshman year will not be as effective during the senior year. The methods we use to help the athlete continue to progress will be discussed throughout the book.

This book is organized to help you establish an effective year-round athletic performance enhancement program. Chapter 1, Training Philosophy, introduces the concepts we use to address our athletes' needs. Comprehensive athletic performance starts with the purpose because without an understanding of the "why" then the program will be limited. Concepts such as teaching, personal development, programming philosophy, mental conditioning, and player responsibility are discussed.

One of the challenges facing the athletic performance coach is how to demonstrate the effectiveness of the training protocols. In chapter 2, Testing and Evaluation, we address effective tests and protocols used to give an overall picture of the athlete and explain ways to use these measures as an effective feedback tool for the athletes and sport coaches.

No program is complete without an understanding of chapter 3, Nutrition and Recovery. We as athletic performance coaches must view ourselves as demolition experts, possessing the knowledge and skill to systematically tear the body down so it will respond by growing stronger. The time between training sessions is of paramount importance if you want to maximize the effectiveness of the protocols. Without proper recovery you may find yourself in an undesirable position.

In chapter 4, Warm-Up and Flexibility, we address how to prepare for upcoming activity. These movements will take the body through a full range of motion to improve flexibility and warm the body. We discuss additional concepts that can be incorporated into the warm-up to enhance the training of the complete football player.

Chapters 5 and 6 focus on movement through training programs designed to improve speed, quickness, and agility. It's no secret that better moving athletes are a lot easier to develop into better football players, and these two chapters encompass the drills needed to achieve this. Speed, quickness, and agility training are key factors for football player development. Learn the drills in these chapters and it will make an immediate impact with your performance on the field by developing athleticism.

What's in a coach's toolbox? Chapters 7 and 8 contain exercise descriptions for power and strength exercises. These exercises have been chosen because of their ability to prepare football players to become more athletic by improving total, upper, lower, and core strength, power, mobility, and stability.

Conditioning is a crucial component to the sport of football. Chapter 9 contains various general conditioning drills with appropriate completion and rest times to get the best results. We will also introduce play drives, a more sport-specific conditioning drill that mimics a game drive with runs of various lengths in succession with rest between runs similar to the play clock. These drills were chosen as they develop anaerobic power, the main system used during football.

During the year-round process of training a football player, the training periods are unique to the game itself. No other sport is quite like it. Chapters 10, 11, and 12 break the yearly process into distinct periods of training.

A unique aspect of *Complete Conditioning for Football* is the DVD that compliments, enhances, and supplements the information and exercises within the book. Look for the DVD icon, which is placed next to the exercises that are included in the DVD. Designed to visually demonstrate the more technical aspects of selected drills and exercises, the DVD depicts how to start and complete the exercises with proper technique and intensity as well as variations to be incorporated. When combined with the information in the book, you will have a better understanding of how to structure an athletic performance program that will meet team and individual needs.

Acknowledgments

The two most important coaches in my early development were Coach Brock of the little league Eastside Cowboys and Coach Rowland at Cass Technical High School in Detroit, Michigan. These two men taught me discipline, accountability, and leadership.

I would like to thank the University of Missouri and Head Football Coach Gary Pinkel, who have assisted me with the opportunity to carry out my passion for coaching. Dave Redding, Russ Ball, Dave Toub, Donnie Sommer, and Jeff Fish, former head strength coaches at the University of Missouri, have all left great legacies, and I am honored to be following in their footsteps. I also would like to thank the Mizzou Athletic Performance family for their loyalty, tireless work ethic each day, and their contributions.

My family has been wonderfully supportive of all my endeavors. I would like to thank my parents, Alton and Alma Ivey, for their continuous investment in our family. I am especially thankful for my wife, Starla, and my daughters, Paisli and Serena, without whom I could not accomplish my goals.

Pat Ivey

Sport and the development that is required to play has long been a personal passion, and I am grateful to every single coach I played for and worked with along the way. I know a part of my coaching today can be traced back to my experiences with each of them.

I would like to thank Head Football Coach Gary Pinkel for the model he provides and his assistance in carrying out the job of strength and conditioning every day. The University of Missouri has a history of tremendous strength and conditioning coaches, and it is an honor to be part of that. Pat Ivey has been a tremendous influence in my career and I am grateful. To the Mizzou Athletic Performance family, I say thank you for your passion and influence in my development as well. I am appreciative of the efforts of Alan Edwards and the late Russ Sharp for putting me on the path to a career in strength and conditioning. I would also like to thank Charlie Dudley for taking a chance and giving me an opportunity early in my career.

My family's dedication and care drives me to be the best each day. I would like to thank my parents, Doug Stoner and the late Rosanda Patterson, as well as my stepmother, Linda Stoner, for all that they provided and continue to provide. I am thankful for the influence of my wife, Christin, and her passion for improvement. Finally, my sons, Jarrett and Jackson, are my MVPs and inspire me to provide the best to each athlete.

Josh Stoner

Part I

PROGRAM FEATURES

Chapter 1

Training Philosophy

At first glance, it may seem that no two football training philosophies are alike. The pursuit of wisdom is the key in developing teaching and training philosophies. Experience, teachers, environment, means, and more, are variables in the development of a training philosophy. Organizing these variables into a cohesive set of beliefs, concepts, and attitudes is the challenge. This book represents more than a decade of pursuing wisdom and organizing our beliefs, concepts, and attitudes to develop a complete program for training football players. This program begins with the following mission statement:

- To provide a staff of role models who encourage healthy behavior by example and educate with enthusiasm in an environment that is positive and intense, thereby improving athletic performance and reducing the risk of injury.

- To provide sport-, position-, and individual-specific strength and conditioning programs for football while implementing programs based on sound physiological principles and proven methods to prepare student-athletes for competition.

- To provide sound sport nutrition counseling and education for football players based on scientifically proven methods for performance and recovery.

- To offer a staff committed to providing the student-athlete an environment that promotes academics, social responsibility, and competitive excellence by fostering team cohesiveness and mental toughness through a creative, disciplined approach to training.

COACH'S RESPONSIBILITIES

Delineating the responsibilities of all assistant coaches is the job of the head football coach. The head coach also establishes the football program's teaching and training philosophies. The strength and conditioning program should be designed with this in mind.

Your job as a coach is to help athletes develop and reach their potential. You are measured by results, and your effort determines this. Motivate players to work out and perform at a championship level regardless of age by establishing weight room guidelines and ensuring that each athlete abides by them. You should emphasize constantly how each athlete's development is vital to the team's success by establishing a goal-oriented program. Always communicate well in all facets of the program.

TEACHING PHILOSOPHY

As a coach, be sure to let your players know that you care about them. Understand that trust is earned, not guaranteed. Always lead by example (character) and be a good role model to your players (integrity). By being honest, respectful, and loyal, you will develop and maintain credibility with your players.

Find ways to get your athletes to believe that you are the best coach and teacher in the world. If the athletes believe it, then you will be successful. Always work to be a great teacher. Your teaching is evaluated by your athletes' performances. Keep things simple and don't overcoach. Find the best way to teach each athlete. Teach fundamentals and technique first so they understand them and execute them in every set and every rep. Coach before and after, not during, the set. Give one- and two-word cues during the set.

As a coach, you should always be willing to learn. Look for ways to improve your teaching and methods by seeking out areas for professional development.

When meeting with athletes, start from scratch by covering the basics. Be on time for every meeting; never be late. Always be thoroughly prepared, and have a plan for each meeting. Be professional and have your athletes come prepared to take notes. It is best to find an office or meeting room for the meeting and to keep the door closed.

It is important to watch your language in the weight room. Avoid physical confrontations and never lay a hand on an athlete.

You should always display great enthusiasm and energy. Explain to the players that your role is to critique performance so they do not take your critiques as personal attacks. Find behaviors to be positive about, and build on them. Your communication with your players should be positive and motivating. If it is not, then seek out ways to change.

Consistency is key to establishing and maintaining credibility. Athletes will notice any inconsistency in your interactions. Demand 100 percent effort every workout, every set, every rep. Everyone in the program needs to pay attention to detail. Demand that your athletes compete in all facets of their workouts and against their own standards.

Make sure you are a hard worker at all times. Coach every exercise. Do not stand in one spot with your hands in your pockets, arms folded, leaning against a machine. Be involved. Don't stand around and watch others coach. If you stand around, so will the athletes. Give coaching points before or after the set, or set up another time to give special instructions.

You have an obligation to the athletes, and your energy should be directed toward them. Never laugh or make fun of an athlete in a manner that is harmful or degrading. Never issue unwarranted threats. Instead, try to build up your athletes after adversity such as a tough practice or criticism. Walk-ons and average athletes should be treated like scholarship and star athletes—with respect. Make a conscious effort to get to know all of your players. Remember that all athletes need attention, especially injured athletes. Try to help injured athletes work through the injury both physiologically and psychologically.

You will develop self-starters and leaders by explaining the importance of team, promoting good work habits and the principle of individual accountability, giving players more responsibility such as leading stretching or talking to the team, encouraging positive peer pressure, and constantly emphasizing expectations through positive communication. When athletes understand, they will perform better.

PERSONAL DEVELOPMENT

Seeking out areas for personal development is critical in the path to excellence for both coaches and athletes. Everyone should ask himself, What is my learning plan? What have I invested? How many books have I read lately? Here are some things coaches and athletes can do in the area of personal development:

- Seek out and schedule visits to universities, private training facilities, and professional sport venues, as well as to medical and scientific resources. Visit universities and professional sport clubs. Consult with orthopedic doctors and athletic trainers to understand the nature of injuries. Be creative in finding avenues of opportunity. Not all educational activities cost money.

- Improve your knowledge of strength and conditioning. Research various recovery techniques by visiting massage therapists and specialists in active release techniques (ART), cryotherapy, e-stim, and other technologies. Expand your knowledge of proper nutrition. Seek out a variety of training methods.

- Expand your knowledge beyond the basic requirements of your job or sport. Learn about psychology, leadership, management, and communication. Understand the administrative process and the greater campus community and how it affects athletics.

PLAYERS' RESPONSIBILITIES

To get the best from their coaches, athletes must recognize the areas in which they can improve. These improvements happen only when athletes and coaches work together to make the team successful. The following advice to athletes is adapted from *In Pursuit of Excellence* (3rd edition) by Terry Orlick.

1. Help your coach understand what works best for you and your performance. A common misconception is that the players and coaches are battling each other. This is detrimental to the ultimate team goal. Performance is enhanced when coaches and athletes work together to create a positive environment and share responsibility for pursuing the mission and improving communication.

2. Improve your communication skills. Reacting defensively and shutting down when you are coached is not constructive. Coaching is not always negative. When you are addressed on an issue concerning your attitude or performance, listen first; then engage in a constructive conversation. Understand the coach's point of view, and ask questions to improve your understanding.

3. Take responsibility for your performance. Now that you have listened and understand what changes are necessary, take responsibility for the plan of action.

4. Develop your capacity to direct and control your own focus and actions. Motivate yourself. Be determined to achieve success. The simple fact that your team depends on you should be highly motivating. Trust that the coaching staff works hard to prepare you to be in the best position on game day. If game day comes and you need a rousing speech or the roar of a crowd to get motivated, you are already behind.

PROGRAM PHILOSOPHY AND OBJECTIVES

Any athletic performance program must be guided by sound principles to allow the coaches and players to accomplish their goals and objectives. Everyone must be dedicated to the program and each training session to achieve goals, including the ultimate goal of delivering the best competitive performance.

These are the objectives of a successful athletic performance program:

- Enhance sport performance by improving strength, speed, power, agility, flexibility, body composition, nutrition, and conditioning.
- Reduce the risk of injury. Healthy muscles and joints experience reduced risks of injury. When an injury occurs, a well-conditioned, well-trained athlete will recover faster and spend less time in limited participation than will a poorly trained one.
- Develop mental toughness demonstrated by a high level of focus, maturity, accountability, discipline, competitiveness, and a genuine commitment to the team.
- Minimize distractions and deterrents to personal and team performance.
- Increase confidence. Physical and mental gains will excite athletes and give them the confidence that they can compete against anyone and succeed.

A well-rounded athletic performance program should develop overall body strength. It should address specificity in training by emphasizing hip and core strength and explosiveness with correct technique, while also stimulating muscles at various angles and intensity levels. Multijoint exercises should predominate in workouts, and the overall program should emphasize exercise variation. Complementary exercises will improve athleticism.

MENTAL CONDITIONING

Mental conditioning is broken down into five skill categories: learning to think right, engaging in positive self-talk, reaching optimal arousal, concentrating, and displaying confidence. Football players must use these skills from the whistle to the snap. Just like any other skills, these can be learned and improved with practice. The more you practice these skills, the better focused you will be. A better-focused athlete is a higher-performing athlete.

- **Learning to think right** starts with the simple understanding that wrong (negative) thoughts hurt sport performance and right (positive) thoughts help it. If you have negative thoughts, all you have to do is replace them with positive thoughts. Thinking right is a choice you can make. Keep in mind that no one can make you think anything; you are responsible for your thoughts.
- **Positive self-talk** is the kind of conversation you should be having with yourself, which is the most important one of all. You have to control your own self-talk; if it is wrong, you have to change it. Positive affirmations are a useful tool to control your self-talk. Because self-talk

affects your emotions and your actions, how you think affects how you play.

• **The right level of arousal** requires having composure, which means being in control of yourself. Optimal arousal is reflected in a state of physiological and psychological well-being. An arousal level that is too high or too low will have a negative impact on your performance. Because optimal arousal varies by individual, you must determine your own level. Reaching your own unique arousal level is a skill that you must practice.

• **Concentration** is about finding the right information and staying focused on it. Because most of the information available to you is irrelevant, you have to seek out the information that matters. You get information from what you see, hear, smell, taste, and touch. Concentration is thinking right, and distraction is thinking wrong. It is a choice as well as a skill. Establishing a routine can help.

• **Confidence** is about believing that you are going to deliver your best performance and not focusing on the outcome. It is the opposite of doubt, anxiety, fear, and worry. It is a choice you make by becoming competent. Like concentration, confidence is both a skill and a choice, and it can be developed over time.

In football, the average play lasts six seconds. The most important part of the game happens between the whistle, which indicates the end of the play, and the snap, which is the start of the next play, usually a period of 20 to 40 seconds. During the whistle-to-the-snap period, successful players use the skills of right thinking, positive self-talk, optimal arousal, concentration, and confidence to improve their performance during the next play. You must learn to park the last play and get ready for the next play during this time. Regardless of the results of the play, if you choose to hold on to it, it could have a negative effect on the next play. The ability to deactivate and reactivate is a skill, as is the ability to focus and refocus. The better you use your time from the whistle to the snap, the better you will be from the snap to the whistle.

PR PARADIGM

To achieve mental toughness, you need to understand the concept of the personal record (PR). We emphasize the PR and use it as a driving force to lift each student-athlete to greater levels of performance. Use the PR to create competition with yourself to achieve increases in strength, power, speed, agility, conditioning, and flexibility. The team will improve only as each student-athlete does. This will occur only when all student-athletes are constantly striving to set and break PRs. (See the PR paradigm in figure 1.1.) As the performance of an individual athlete improves, the team's performance improves, creating a new sense of focus and drive for other athletes. When most team members are breaking PRs, eventually, performance will reach championship caliber because of the level of performance required to break PRs.

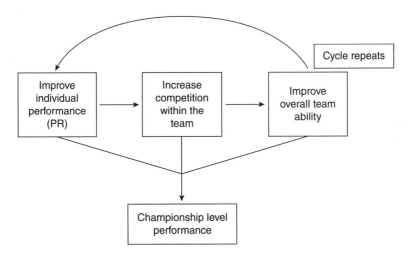

Figure 1.1   The PR paradigm.

MULTILEVEL SYSTEM

We have developed a multilevel system approach to training with an extensive testing and evaluation protocol. With traditional linear periodization, it was becoming increasingly more difficult to illicit gains without plateaus over an athlete's career. While pursuing our quest for maximal strength, we discovered the need for a progressive program (the strength continuum; see figure 1.2) that would take an incoming freshman from learning basic movements to producing and absorbing maximal force while reducing the risk of injury.

Figure 1.2   The strength continuum.

Athletes who had been training with the same program for four or five years were lacking the motivation and enthusiasm necessary to compete at a championship level. The standards we chose to integrate as guidelines became paramount in how athletes progressed. We used statistical analysis to determine the relationships among an athlete's strength, power, and speed as a way to determine whether the athlete was ready to progress to the next level. All athletes now start at level zero and may or may not progress to level four based on their performance and leadership abilities over their careers. Level five is the professional player development program.

Level Zero

All incoming players begin at this level. Athletes learn the basic movement skills that will form a strong foundation for their careers. General physical preparedness (GPP) is targeted through the use of body weight exercises. The functional movement screen (see chapter 2) is used to identify areas in which athletes are weak, deficient, or immobile. Mental preparation for the demands of the succeeding levels also is emphasized at this level.

Many different body weight exercises are performed at this level. Athletes are taught to depend on each other through individual performances; if expectations are not met, the group repeats the exercise.

GENERAL GOALS OF LEVEL ZERO

- Identify areas for improvement through the functional movement screening.
- Increase the athlete's work capacity.
- Introduce team concepts.

Level One

The functional movement screening is used at level zero to identify areas in which athletes are weak or immobile. At level one, exercises are prescribed to improve these areas. Improvements in foundation exercises—Bench Press, Back Squat, and Hang Clean—are emphasized. General physical preparedness (GPP) is targeted through various techniques such as submaximal eccentrics and the modified repetition method.

In level one, we limit exercise selection to emphasize learning technique. Most changes are to repetition schemes, which are done for proper motor learning. The introduction of all of these new movements at once is a great shock to the central nervous system (CNS), and the athlete must be allowed to adapt. At this level, testing focuses on the 5-repetition max (5RM) at 85 percent as the athlete learns. True max effort could lead to poor technique and possibly injury.

GENERAL GOALS OF LEVEL ONE

- Learn proper lifting technique for the Back Squat, Bench Press, and Hang Clean.
- Improve joint mobility.
- Learn to differentiate between hip and back extension in Olympic lifts so more work can be done on the Hang Clean to develop explosiveness.

Level Two

Players at level two have met the expectations and goals of levels zero and one. Generally, those who begin on-campus training during the summer will be at level two in the fall. Players who begin in the fall or spring may be able to move to level two after four to eight weeks at levels zero and one.

At level two, the athlete will be able to differentiate between hip and back extension on the Olympic lifts. This foundation will pay greater dividends in the future so he can make greater progress on the Olympic lifts. With the proper technique established at level one, the athlete will be able to spend more time increasing max strength. He will have a greater work capacity and will be able to handle a greater total volume in future workouts. The addition of supplemental exercises will increase the overall volume of workouts. Testing at this level still uses 5RM at 85 percent because the athlete is still learning. This will help to improve lean body mass.

GENERAL GOALS OF LEVEL TWO

- Continue to increase work capacity.
- Increase max voluntary strength.
- Improve body composition by increasing lean mass.

Level Three

This level consists mainly of second- and third-year players. Players at this level will have approached and even exceeded some conference standards (see chapter 2, Testing and Evaluation). Players at this level demonstrate the capacity to be self-starters, have reciprocated trust with the staff, and can maintain a positive attitude.

To continue gaining maximal strength, the athlete must change the way he performs the movements (Back Squat, Bench Press, and so on) to give his body a new stimulus to adapt to. This can be done with isometrics, eccentrics, and other methods. Some special exercises are added to teach the muscles to better absorb force. The athlete will do various types of jumps, eccentrics, and isometrics to learn force absorption. This is important because the more force the muscles can absorb, the more effective an athlete will become at producing force. The athlete will begin to use the Tendo unit for Hang Clean testing. The athlete can learn new movements more quickly because of what he learned at levels one and two. The more movements the athlete learns, the more the learning curve increases. At this level, the ability to learn new movements easily will lead to greater motor learning, which can enhance play on the field. The combination of these new methods will dramatically improve performance testing and the potential for improvements in skill play. The athlete will learn to perform the core lifts at intensities over 90 percent. This will teach him how to recruit more available motor units, which will lead to greater strength gains and the ability to call on more units for activities such as running and jumping.

GENERAL GOALS OF LEVEL THREE

- Continue increasing max voluntary strength.
- Introduce the dynamic effort method and the use of the Tendo (see chapter 7).
- Increase the ability of muscles to absorb force and improve eccentric capability.
- Increase the number of movement patterns.
- Increase the strength of the stretch reflex (explosion).

Level Four

This program is designed for athletes who have exceeded a majority of conference standards. Most of these will be fourth- and fifth-year players. Depending on physical maturity, some third-year players may be at level four. Players at level four must lead by example and possess a positive, warrior-like mentality. They must be able to prepare mentally for each workout and demonstrate the highest level of focus. Level-four athletes are expected to motivate others as well.

At this point, an athlete's musculoskeletal system has been well trained and is approaching the top end of where it needs to be for football. Now, to enhance on-the-field results, other biological systems, primarily the central nervous system (CNS), need to be trained. Training will make the CNS more effective. The dynamic strength component will increase, allowing the athlete to generate more force in less time (rate of force development), thereby increasing functional strength on the playing field. Motor recruitment abilities will be increased through true max effort work. Max effort (1RM) work will force the body to use more motor units at any given time. The more motor units trained to perform at one time, the more the athlete can call on them at any time, which will lead to greater strength gains and more units available for activities such as running and jumping. (For any 1RM attempts, two additional spotters will be at each end of the bar.) Special strength training allows the athlete to work on areas of weakness (e.g., starting strength, static strength, accelerative strength, reversal strength), because those areas can now be readily identified.

Level-four athletes can learn movements at a higher level than others can, so the effort of their core exercises must be changed every one to three weeks. The adaptation of the auxiliary lifts is so refined that the exercise selection should be changed nearly weekly to prevent burnout. Again, the more movement patterns they learn, the greater their ability to learn more movement patterns will be. Because dynamic strength and most special strengths require moving a lighter weight at a higher velocity, less mechanical energy is expended, so more time and energy are available for refining sport skills. At this level, the Tendo unit is often used to make sure that the loading is proper for the type of strength being trained.

GENERAL GOALS OF LEVEL FOUR

- Enhance dynamic strength through the use of chains and bands.
- Increase motor recruitment (true max effort equals 1RM).
- Refine special strengths such as starting, acceleration, and reversing.
- Further increase the number of movement patterns.

Level Five

The goal of level five is to prepare an athlete for the NFL Combine and Pro Day. Level five is no longer solely for the sport; it prepares the athlete for the 40-Yard Dash, I-Test, Three-Cone, Broad Jump, Vertical Jump, and 225 Reps test. To succeed at this level, the athlete must become stronger, faster, and quicker. The body adapts more quickly as it gains experience through training. To keep the body from reaching a plateau, a great variety of exercises are used on effort days along with different methods for doing the exercises through the addition of implements such as chains and bands. Bands and chains are added to dynamic effort and special exercises as well. Bands are heavily used on the Box Squat and Bench Press because they add an overspeed eccentric and a resisted concentric, which force the body to learn to move even faster than with dynamic work. The athlete learns to move his entire body through space more rapidly, which translates into more reps in the 225 test, a higher vertical jump, a longer broad jump, and a decrease in time for the performance tests. Some of the methods used at level five are very taxing on the CNS. A player at level five training should not engage in other sports or in other forms of training because of the increased risk of overtraining.

Chapter 2

Testing and Evaluation

Testing and evaluation are integral to a football training program. Knowing exactly where the team is in terms of achievement and maintaining historical data for reference assists in the evaluation of a program. Every year's statistics can be compared to past years' statistics. There are 14 test or measurement categories, including anthropometric, strength, speed, agility, and flexibility.

The number-one challenge in evaluating 14 areas is scheduling the time. With this number of evaluations, testing typically takes one and a half to two weeks to complete, depending on the number of days per week given for training. Examples of specific testing calendars are presented at the end of the chapter.

Another challenging aspect of testing and evaluation is timing, testing when the athletes are ready to peak. Athletes may prepare well in anticipation of a designated testing period, but be unready to show their hard work as a result of other factors. For this reason, we have instituted the PR system discussed in chapter 1 (page 8). This allows athletes to display their best whenever they are ready as long as it fits within the structure of the program. For example, if we are testing 225 reps in week 8 and an athlete sets a personal record in week 6, it counts. Athletes have set personal records in week 1 that have counted toward that training cycle. This system establishes an environment that is intrinsically motivating because athletes know that they will be allowed to demonstrate their best whenever they are ready. Overall, much of the success of our strength and conditioning program has been driven by our extensive testing and evaluation program. Follow the checklist shown in figure 2.1 to develop an effective testing program.

Step 1: Outline Testing

- Check the availability of the facility two weeks prior to testing. Is it available? If not, what is plan B?
- Check batteries, bolts, connections, and so on. Is all equipment in working order?
- Determine the length of the testing calendar. How many days do you have to test the team?
- Determine the tests you are going to administer. What will you test the team on?
- Set up a testing outline. Plug in the tests to the days of the week. Cross-reference the training schedule to make sure the plan will work.

Step 2: Organize Procedures and Personnel

- Determine testing procedures. How will the tests be administered?
- Delegate staff. Who will assist in testing, and what are their responsibilities?
- Educate assisting staff. Meet to cover how the data will be collected and transferred to the master profile.
- Prepare the assisting staff. Make sure each assisting staff member has an updated profile, clipboard, pen or pencil, projected max chart (kilo, standard), updated injury report, and any individual notes of importance.

Step 3: Collect Data

- Stress accuracy. Make sure all tests are watched and all data are recorded. Staff must be focused and see every test set. If a test is not seen, the athlete will have to repeat the test. Staff must do everything possible to avoid having an athlete repeat a set.
- Gather results on every test. It is important to write down everything on the master profile. There should never be blanks on any test. Athletes who cannot test will be excused by the athletic trainer.

Step 4: Break Down Testing Site

- Break down and clean up all testing setup areas (equipment, duct tape, cones, etc.).

Step 5: Update Player Profile

- Insert a row for new test data with the date of the test period—for example, off-season 3/20.
- Record all new results on the player profile. Make sure the athlete's class status is accurate.
- For any tests not performed because of injury, list the injury (knee, hip, etc.) on the profile under that test.
- Have other staff members review the profile for accuracy (inch marks, periods, etc.) before distributing it to sport coaches.
- Turn in player profile results to the sport coaches within 24 hours of the last test.
- Prepare a highlight sheet of performance increases—for example, team vertical average up 2 inches.

Step 6: Update Team Record Board

- Update any new team records and include the date.
- Update the new top three performers from that testing period.

Step 7: Evaluate

- Evaluate the program used for that training period. Make notes to improve the workout design for the next time (% schemes, set and rep cycles, off days, peaks and valleys in performance, total PRs, top performers, etc.).

Figure 2.1   Testing checklist.

GOAL SHEETS

Prior to every testing and evaluation period, individual goal sheets (see figure 2.2 for an example) are printed for athletes to fill out. A coach sits down with the athlete to discuss his goals and methods to achieve those goals. Once both parties agree, both athlete and coach sign the goal sheet and a copy is made for the athlete to keep. After the testing period is over, the coach sits down with the athlete again and calculates the percentage of goals achieved. The primary reward is the satisfaction received from achieving goals. The objective is to make the goals attainable; however, some athletes prefer to set their goals really high even if they achieve only some and not all of them.

MASTER PROFILE

A player profile (see figure 2.3 for an example) is kept to record an athlete's progress throughout his career. Every testing period, a new line for data entry is created using an Excel spreadsheet. Across the top of the spreadsheet are the categories of testing and evaluation. The profile is separated by offense and defense and then by position (OL, TE, RB, WR, QB, DT, DE, LB, safeties, CB, and kickers and punters). All PRs are bolded, and standards are highlighted. Each player's individual goals are on the bottom line of his section for quick reference.

STANDARDS

Standards are in place for 10 out of the 14 areas we test and evaluate, including body composition, all strength-based tests (Bench Press, Squat, Hang Clean, and 225 Reps), power (Vertical Jump and Standing Broad Jump), agility (Pro Agility and Three-Cone), and linear speed (40-Yard Dash). We derived our standards (table 2.1, page 20) from past NFL Combine results, past testing results, and data from other schools. Each position has its own standards. These standards give athletes goals to strive for and provide constant motivation. Whenever an athlete achieves a standard, he is recognized immediately by teammates and staff. A bell is near the center of the weight room for the athletes to ring every time they achieve a PR that is at or above the standard.

Name/Date	St. #	Height	Weight	Body Fat %	Bench Press	Squat	Hang Clean	225 Reps	Vertical Jump	Broad Jump	Pull-Up	FMS Score	Sit and reach/ V-sit Flexibility	I-Test	Three-Cone	40-Yard Dash
Conference standards				22.00	400	600	375/260	26	28"	8'6"		14		4.8 s	7.7 s	5.3 s
Name/Class																
Postseason 11/12		6046	242	23.70	247	282	155	3	21.6"	7'3.5"	NT	NA	5/13.75/5 = +13.75"	NT	NT	NT
Off-season 3/13	2	6050	247	22.50	265	312	200	6	21.9"	7'7"	2	NA	4/13.75/6 = +11.75"	4.93	7.94	5.38
Preseason 7/13	2	NT	259	24.00	300	353	226	10	23.3"	7'9.25"	5	NA	4/13.5/7.5 = +10"	4.90	7.89	NT
Postseason 11/13		NT	254	25.70	Wrist	359	Wrist	Wrist	24.1"	7'6.25"	NT	NA	3/14/7.75 = +9.25"	NT	NT	NT
Off-season 3/14	4	6052	260	26.70	Wrist	Wrist	Wrist	Wrist	25.5"	81"	Wrist	NA	2/14.75/8 = +8.75"	4.73	7.78	5.31
Preseason 7/14	4	NT	270	26.70	300	365	239	10	26.6"	7'9"	3	15	6.75/13.25 = -6.5"	4.89	7.58	NT
Postseason 11/14		NT	265	27.40	300-Wr.	347	227	12	25.7"	7'7.5"	NT	14	7.25/10 = -2.75"	NT	NT	NT
Off-season 3/15	4	6057	265	25.70	306	370	246	13	24.2"	7'6"-Ft.	6	13	7.5/9.5 = -2"	4.81	7.73	5.30
Preseason 7/15																
Goals for period				24.00	325	400	275	15	28"	8'3"	10	14		4.6s	7.7s	NT
Results for period																
Percentage achieved																
/12	=	%														

I agree with the above strength and conditioning goals that I and the strength and conditioning department have established. I hereby make the commitment to the focus, intensity, enthusiasm, leadership, and determination necessary to achieve my goals. My goals will be achieved by _____ (date).

Player's signature _____ Date _____

Strength and conditioning coach's signature _____ Date _____

Figure 2.2 Goal sheets are designed with the input of both the coach and the athlete. This player's personal records (PRs) are bolded; standards are highlighted.

Name/Date	St. #	Height	Weight	Body Fat %	Bench Press	Squat	Hang Clean	225 Reps	Vertical Jump	Broad Jump	Pull-Up	FMS Score	Sit and Reach/V-Sit Flexibility	I-Test	Three-Cone	40-Yard Dash
Offensive line																
Conference standards				22.00	400	600	375/260	26	28"	8'6"		14		4.8 s	7.7 s	5.3 s
Name/Class																
Postseason 11/12		6046	242	23.70	247	282	155	3	21.6"	7'3.5"	NT	NA	5/13.75/5 = +13.75"	NT	NT	NT
Off-season 3/13	2	6050	247	**22.50**	265	312	200	6	21.9"	7'7"	2	NA	4/13.75/6 = +11.75"	4.93	7.94	5.38
Preseason 7/13	2	NT	259	24.00	300	353	226	10	23.3"	7'9.25"	5	NA	4/13.5/7.5 = +10"	4.90	7.89	NT
Postseason 11/13		NT	254	25.70	Wrist	359	Wrist	Wrist	24.1"	7'6.25"	NT	NA	3/14/7.75 = +9.25"	NT	NT	NT
Off-season 3/14	4	6052	260	26.70	Wrist	Wrist	Wrist	Wrist	25.5"	**8'1"**	Wrist	NA	2/14.75/8 = +8.75"	**4.73**	7.78	5.31
Preseason 7/14	4	NT	270	26.70	300	365	239	10	**26.6"**	7'9"	3	**15**	6.75/13.25 = −6.5"	4.89	**7.58**	NT
Postseason 11/14		NT	265	27.40	300-Wr.	347	227	12	25.7"	7'7.5"	NT	14	7.25/10 = −2.75"	NT	NT	NT
Off-season 3/15	4	6057	265	25.70	**306**	**370**	**246**	**13**	24.2"	7'6"-Ft.	**6**	13	**7.5/9.5 = −2"**	4.81	7.73	**5.30**
Preseason 7/15																
Goals for 2015				25.00	325	400	230	14	28"	8'3"	6	14	0"	4.65	7.70	5.30
Name/Class																
Off-season 3/15	0	6046	264	**30.60**	**281**	Knee	**268**	**7**	Knee	Knee	**1**	**12**	**0/10 = −10"**	Knee	Knee	**5.62**
Preseason 7/15																
Goals for 2015																
Name/Class																
Preseason 7/13	3	6054	281	**19.30**	341	447	285	16	26.5"	8'6"	8	NA	6/9.5/10.5 = +5"	4.69	7.83	NT
Postseason 11/13		NT	294	21.60	353	459	336	20	27.6"	8'4"	NT	NA	6/9/11 = +4"	NT	NT	NT
Off-season 3/14	7	6054	294	19.60	359	517	375	19	28.4"	8'10.5"	11	NA	4.25/9/11.25 = +2"	4.50	7.43	5.10
Preseason 7/14	6	NT	303	22.60	**360**	535	**381**	**21**	30.1"	8'9.5"	**14**	15	11/8.75 = +2.25"	4.44	7.47	NT
Off-season 3/15	6	6055	295	20.00	348	**582**	239	20	**32.1"**	**9'0"**	14	**17**	**12.75/0 = +12.75"**	**4.33**	**7.35**	**5.03**
Preseason 7/15																
Goals for 2015			300	19.20	400	600	385	23	31"	9'	1		4"	4.40	7.40	5.00

Figure 2.3 Sample master profile of three players. Each player's PRs are bolded; standards are highlighted.

19

Table 2.1   Physical Standards for College-Level Football Players

Position	Body Fat %	Bench Press	Squat	Hang Clean Levels One and Two	Hang Clean Levels Three and Four	225 Reps	Vertical Jump	Broad Jump	Pro Agility	Three-Cone	40-Yard Dash
Offensive line	22%	400	600	375	260	26	28"	8'6"	4.8 s	7.7 s	5.3 s
Tight end	12%	350	550	350	245	20	32"	9'3"	4.5 s	7.2 s	4.8 s
Running back	9%	330	450	335	235	16	35"	10'0"	4.4 s	7.1 s	4.5 s
Receiver	8%	310	450	320	225	12	37"	10'0"	4.1 s	7.0 s	4.5 s
Quarterback	9%	310	450	325	225	12	32"	9'6"	4.3 s	7.2 s	4.7 s
Defensive tackle	18%	400	600	375	260	28	28"	8'8"	4.7 s	7.7 s	5.1 s
Defensive end	15%	365	550	360	250	23	33"	9'2"	4.4 s	7.4 s	4.8 s
Linebacker	12%	360	525	350	245	22	34"	9'5"	4.3 s	7.2 s	4.7 s
Safety	9%	330	500	335	235	16	35"	10'0"	4.2 s	7.0 s	4.6 s
Corner	8%	310	450	320	225	12	37"	10'0"	4.1 s	6.9 s	4.5 s
Kicker or punter	12%	300	400	275	200	10	34"	9'0"	4.4 s	7.2 s	4.8 s

CLUBS

Clubs (table 2.2) track benchmarks for 7 of the 14 areas we test and evaluate. From year to year, we compare how many athletes in the program achieved a certain level of progress. All club information is recorded and inserted into a bar graph for easy analysis. When examined yearly, the clubs give us good feedback to help us make program design tweaks from a team perspective.

Table 2.2 Football Clubs

Bench Press (pounds)	300	325	350	375	400	425	450	500
Squat (pounds)	400	450	500	550	600	650	700	750
Hang Clean (pounds)	300	325	350	375	400+			
Speed Clean (pounds)	225	250	275	300	325	350		
225 Reps (pounds)	10	15	20	25	30+			
Vertical Jump (inches)	30" to 34.9"	35" to 39.9"	40" or more					
Broad Jump (feet and inches)	9' to 9'5.75"		9'6" to 9'11.75"		10' to 10'11.75"		11' or more	
40-Yard Dash (seconds)	4.9	4.8	4.7	4.6	4.5	4.4	4.3	

PR PERCENTAGE

Calculating the PR percentage (PR%) is a way to measure the achievement of the team. The goal is to determine what percentage of the team is setting personal records. We want at least 80 percent of the team setting personal records or achieving the standard in the Bench Press, Squat, Hang Clean, 225 Reps, and 40-Yard Dash. We want at least 70 percent of the team setting personal records or achieving the standard in the Vertical Jump, Standing Broad Jump, Pro Agility, and Three-Cone. Remember that for a new program, the PR% will be much higher because those athletes are adapting to new exercises, sets, reps, and percentages, which is the primary reason we created the level system. Each new level introduces new stimuli to prevent plateaus.

GAME DAY IN THE WEIGHT ROOM

We emphasize testing and evaluation dates by labeling them Game Day in the Weight Room. We place a sign in the weight room to inform everyone in the athletic department that it is not just a normal day. Even though we give athletes the chance to set records during the training cycle, we intensify the atmosphere of evaluation days to that of a game day to inspire them to mentally focus on doing the best they can on that particular day during test week.

RETESTING

We allow some retesting for athletes because we want to give them every opportunity to do their best. Some argue that retesting allows athletes to make excuses about not achieving their best performance on the day it matters. We emphasize preparation, which means that every day is important. In most cases, only a few athletes have to retest, mostly as a result of injuries that inhibited training. For power indicators, in particular, we have found that we must allow for delayed transformation effect when retesting. Often we have to tell athletes "no." We are always going to protect athletes first; any personal agendas are secondary. Once the final retest is completed, all new PRs are entered for the next testing period. For instance, PRs set during spring football are included with the summer data collection.

RECORD BOARDS

Record boards kept in the weight room list all-time high performers in each testing category as well as the top three performers from the most recent testing period. Each testing period, we update the board to reflect any changes to school records and the current top three performers. When an athlete breaks a school record in a given category, this is announced along with the PR to the entire training group. This is another tool for motivating athletes.

OFF-SEASON FRIDAY TESTING

Off-season testing is held on the final five weeks of the off-season. The first week, we test the 40-Yard Dash, Vertical Jump, and Pro Agility. The second week includes the 40-Yard Dash (10-Yard Dash for athletes at levels three and four), Standing Broad Jump, and Three-Cone. These two groups of tests are administered every other week. Athletes perform three tests each Friday (figure 2.4).

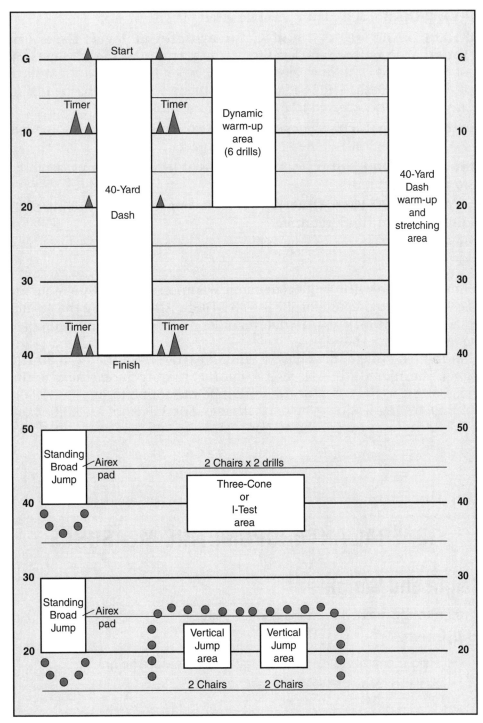

Figure 2.4   Layout for testing performance on a football field. Organization for testing is key.

40-Yard Dash: Each player gets two attempts.

10-Yard Dash (weeks 2 and 4, for athletes at levels three and four): All level-three and level-four athletes run a 10-Yard Dash instead of the 40-Yard Dash in weeks 2 and 4. They get four or five attempts on the 10-Yard Dash. The head athletic trainer also may prescribe this for any athletes not cleared to run the 40-Yard Dash.

Vertical Jump: Each player gets at least two jumps, although some may get more. The test is done on the jump pad.

Standing Broad Jump: Each player gets at least two jumps, although some may get more.

Pro Agility (20-Yard Shuttle): Each player gets at least two attempts, although some may get more.

Three-Cone: Each player gets at least two attempts, although some may get more.

Athletes begin with a general dynamic warm-up followed by a more specific warm-up to prepare for the 40-Yard Dash. After running the 40-Yard Dash, the athlete may test in whatever order he chooses. He must complete the three tests for that day.

An injured athlete must have a written excuse from the head athletic trainer. The injured athlete is responsible for bringing the excuse to testing and giving it to the coach at the station he cannot perform.

A final testing session is held for athletes who have not set a PR on any of the Friday tests except the 40-Yard Dash.

GENERAL ANTHROPOMETRIC MEASURES

Height and Weight

You must be dressed in shorts and a T-shirt.

Equipment

- Height chart and carpenter's square to measure height
- Scale to measure weight

Height

- Remove your shoes.
- Stand tall next to the wall with the height chart with your heels together and your toes out without touching the wall.
- The coach will rest a carpenter's square on top of your head and flush against the wall to obtain your height reading.

Weight

- Remove your shoes and stand on the scale.
- Round down to the nearest pound; for example, record 197.8 pounds as 197 pounds.

Male Body Composition (Skinfold Method)

For the skinfold measurements, obtain duplicate measurements for three sites: chest/pectoral, abdomen, and thigh. Along with the measurements, note age. This is the formula used to find body fat percentage:

Body fat % = {457 / [1.10938 − (0.0008267 × sum of skinfolds) + 0.0000016 × (sum of skinfolds^2)] − (0.000257 × age)} − 414.2

Equipment

- Calipers
- Your profile with previous measurements for body fat
- Three-site skinfold profile from last test

Procedure

- Take all measurements on the right side of the body.
- Place the caliper 1 centimeter away from the thumb and finger, perpendicular to the skinfold and halfway between the crest and the base of the fold.
- Maintain the pinch while taking the reading.
- Wait one or two seconds, but no longer, before reading the caliper.
- Take duplicate measurements at each site, and retest if the measurements are not within 2 millimeters.
- Rotate among measurement sites, or allow time for the skin to regain its normal texture and thickness.

Chest/Pectoral

- Stand still with your arms hanging down at your sides.
- Take the measurement at a diagonal fold, half the distance between the right anterior shoulder and the nipple (figure 2.5*a*).

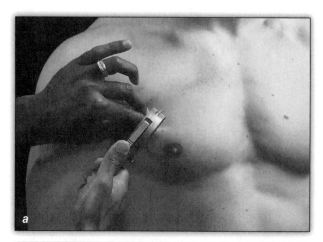

Abdomen

- Stand still with your arms hanging down at your sides.
- Take the measurement at a vertical fold, 2 centimeters to the right of the umbilicus (figure 2.5*b*).

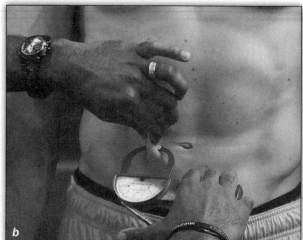

Thigh

- Stand still with your arms hanging down at your sides. Put your right leg in front of your left leg and lean your body weight onto your left leg.
- Take the measurement at a vertical fold on the anterior midline of your thigh, midway between the top border of your patella and your hip crease (figure 2.5*c*).

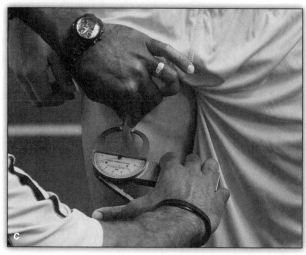

Figure 2.5 Skinfold measurements: *(a)* for the chest/pectoral area; *(b)* for the abdomen; *(c)* for the thigh.

EXPLOSIVE STRENGTH

5-Repetition Hang Clean Max

Before you attempt this test, the coach checks that the weight you are going to attempt will be a new rep max PR if you can perform the lift successfully.

Equipment

- Projected max chart
- Most recent profile

Procedure

- Begin in the upright position, feet shoulder-width apart, hands palms down, gripping the bar outside the thighs.
- As the coach looks on, attempt to lift a maximum designated weight five times. (See chapter 7, page 113, for a more detailed description of the Hang Clean.)
- For a repetition to count, you must complete the lift with the bar resting on your anterior deltoids and your elbows high in a fully extended standing position.
- Following the completion of 5 reps, the coach determines whether you should attempt a heavier weight or terminate the test. The coach may terminate the test at any time.
- After you have successfully completed 5 reps, the coach determines the 1-rep max by consulting the projected max chart. On the workout card, the coach records the weight used and the number of successful repetitions as well as the projected 1RM.

3- and 1-Repetition Speed Hang Clean Max

Before you attempt this test, the coach checks that the weight you are going to attempt will be a new rep max PR if you can perform the lift successfully.

Equipment

- Projected max chart
- Most recent profile
- Tendo unit

Procedure

- Begin in the upright position, feet shoulder-width apart, hands gripping the bar outside the thighs.
- As the coach looks on, attempt to lift a designated weight at 1.55 m/s for 3 reps (level three) or 1 rep (level four).
- For a repetition to count, you must complete the lift with the bar resting on your anterior deltoids, elbows high, in a fully extended starting position.
- After the completion of the test, the coach determines whether you should attempt a heavier weight or terminate the test. The coach may terminate the test at any time.
- After you have successfully completed 3 reps (level three) or 1 rep (level four), the coach determines the 1-rep max by consulting the projected max chart.

VERTICAL EXPLOSIVENESS

Vertical Jump With Jump Pad

Equipment

- Vertical jump pad (If testing on a soft surface such as field turf, place a harder material such as a plywood board underneath the pad.)
- Handheld digital readouts
- Most recent profile

Procedure

- Stand on the back of the jump pad with your heels on the edge of the pad (figure 2.6*a*).
- Attempt to jump as high as possible while reaching up for a target placed above the pad (figure 2.6*b*). If you attempt to tuck your knees during the jump or land in a squat, the jump is disqualified.
- You must control your landing and land on two feet (figure 2.6*c*).
- You are allowed multiple attempts. The number of repetitions allowed is determined by monitoring your attempts. When you begin to drop from that day's best jump, fatigue has begun and the test should be terminated. All attempts for the day should be recorded.

Figure 2.6 Vertical Jump With Jump Pad: *(a)* stand on back of jump pad; *(b)* jump as high as possible while reaching for target; *(c)* land on both feet.

Vertical Jump With Vertec

Equipment

- Vertec
- Vane resetter
- Rubber band
- Most recent profile

Procedure

- Align your foot and hip against the side of the Vertec.
- Reach your dominant hand to maximum height. Extraneous motion is not allowed.
- Adjust the Vertec so that the tip of your middle finger is flush with a mark on the Vertec support rod that is 12 to 18 inches below the bottom vane on the Vertec.

Figure 2.7 Vertical Jump With Vertec.

- Stand with your hip beside the Vertec directly under the vanes with the backs of your heels beside the base of the Vertec.
- Attempt two vertical jumps, trying to touch the highest vanes (figure 2.7). Record both attempts.

HORIZONTAL EXPLOSIVENESS

Broad Jump

Equipment

- Duct tape
- Red and black Sharpie markers
- Metal ruler
- Square ruler
- 25-foot measuring tape
- Most recent profile

Procedure

- Stand with your toes behind the starting line.
- Jump forward off both feet for one jump (figure 2.8). If you fall back on your hands or do not stick the landing, you must attempt the broad jump again.
- The coach measures the jump from the heel of the rear-most foot with the ruler flat on the ground.
- You are allowed a minimum of two attempts. The total number of repetitions is determined by monitoring your attempts. When you begin to drop from that day's best jump, fatigue has begun and the test should be terminated. All attempts for the day should be recorded.

Figure 2.8　Broad Jump.

UPPER-BODY STRENGTH

5-Repetition Bench Max

This test evaluates your skill at the Bench Press (page 131). Before you attempt this test, the coach checks your previous max to make sure the weight you are going to attempt will be a new rep max PR if you perform the lift successfully.

Equipment

- Projected max chart
- Most recent profile

Procedure

- Begin with your eyes under the bar, feet flat on the floor, hips down. Individual grips will vary, although usually the grip is wider than shoulder width.
- With a spotter in position and the coach present, attempt to lift a maximum designated weight five times. (See chapter 8, page 131, for a more detailed description of the Bench Press.) The bar must touch your chest at the end of the descent, and your arms must be fully extended at the top of the movement.
- If the spotter touches the bar at any time, the test is terminated. After you have completed 5 repetitions, the coach determines whether you should attempt a heavier weight or terminate the test.
- After your have successfully completed 5 reps, the coach determines the 1-rep max by consulting the projected max chart.

LOWER-BODY STRENGTH

5-Repetition Back Squat Max

Before you attempt this test, the coach checks your previous max to make sure the weight you are going to attempt will be a new rep max PR if you perform the Back Squat (page 122) successfully.

Equipment

- Projected max chart
- Most recent profile

Procedure

- Begin in the upright position with the bar resting on your traps, head up and feet slightly wider than your shoulders with toes pointed slightly outward.
- With a spotter in position and the coach present, attempt to lift a maximum designated weight five times. (See chapter 8, page 122, for a more detailed description of the Back Squat.) You must squat until midthigh is parallel to the floor and must fully extend at the top of the movement for the repetition to count.
- If the spotter helps you at any time during the movement, the test is terminated. The coach has the authority to stop the test at any time.
- After you have completed 5 repetitions, the coach determines whether you should attempt a heavier weight or terminate the test.
- After you have successfully completed 5 reps, the coach determines the 1-rep max by consulting the projected max chart.

UPPER-BODY ENDURANCE

225 Reps

Before you attempt this test, the coach checks your previous PR.

Equipment

- Projected max chart
- Most recent profile

Procedure

- Begin with your eyes under the bar, feet flat on the floor, hips down. Individual grips will vary, although the typical grip is wider than shoulder width.
- Follow a specified warm-up progression based on your 5-rep max PR for the Bench Press. (See chapter 8, page 131, for a more detailed description of the Bench Press.)
- With a spotter in position and the coach present, attempt to Bench Press 225 pounds as many times as possible. The bar must touch your chest at the end of the descent, and your arms must be fully extended at the top of the movement. The coach monitoring the set counts the number of reps you complete.

Max Pull-Ups

Equipment

- Pull-up bar
- Most recent profile

Procedure

- Using a wide grip, begin your first rep fully hanging from the pull-up bar and pull your chin over the bar.
- After the first rep, fully extend your arms during the descent and wait for the "up" call from the coach before making another attempt.
- A rep does not count if you kick excessively, your chin does not come over the bar, or you do not wait for the "up" call. The official counter must be a coach, and he must record the total number of successful attempts.

Max Assisted Pull-Ups

Equipment

- Assisted chin-up machine
- Scale to determine add-on test weight
- Most recent profile

Procedure

- Set 25 percent of your body weight on the machine to test. Use 5-pound and 7.5-pound add-on weights, rounding up to the nearest 2.5 pounds (31.5 pounds would round to 32.5 pounds to add on).
- Your grip may vary from the chin-up to pull-up position, depending on the testing criteria.
- Attempt to do as many reps in the pull-up grip position as possible. You must fully extend your arms during the descent, and your chin must come as high as the grip handles.
- The official counter must be a coach, and he must record the total number of successful attempts.

HIP AND GROIN FLEXIBILITY

V-Sit

Equipment

- Duct tape to denote a specific location for the test to be performed
- Tape measure
- Most recent profile

Procedure

- Remove your shoes.
- Sit flat on the floor where no elevations will alter the path of your legs; spread your legs as wide as possible, toes pointed to the ceiling and knees straight. Cross your arms over your chest and keep your middle finger on top of the acromion process.
- Bring your forehead as close to the floor as possible.
- The coach measures the distance from your forehead to the floor (figure 2.9).
- Your knees must stay straight, and you should have no excessive rotating of the feet inward or outward.

Figure 2.9   V-sit.

Sit and Reach

Equipment

- Sit-and-Reach box
- Most recent profile

Procedure

- Remove your shoes and place the soles of your feet under the box.
- Overlap your hands and reach forward as far as possible (figure 2.10). Your hands must not separate. You must not bend your knees; the coach holds your knees down. Hold your farthest reach for two seconds. The coach records the number in inches past the level of your feet, which is zero. Anything above your feet is recorded as a negative number.
- To calculate the overall score for flexibility, use this formula:

Overall flex score = Sit and Reach score – V-Sit score

The higher the overall number, the better your flexibility.

Figure 2.10   Sit and Reach.

STRAIGHT-AHEAD SPEED

40-Yard Dash

Equipment

- Electronic timer or stopwatches
- Ten 4-inch cones
- Most recent profile

Procedure

- Place two 4-inch cones one foot outside the hash mark on the goal line and at the 10-, 20-, 30-, and 40-yard lines. Set up electronic timers or coaches with handheld stopwatches on the front edges of the 10- and 40-yard lines.

- Begin in a three-point stance with your lead hand on the timing pad just behind the goal line. Begin at your discretion and sprint through the 40-yard line. You must run at least two trials but not exceed four attempts.

- To equate electronic time to stopwatch, research indicates that you need to subtract 0.24 seconds from the time indicated on the electronic readout.

LATERAL SPEED AND AGILITY

Pro Agility

Equipment

- Stopwatch
- Duct tape
- Three 12-inch cones
- One chair
- Three coaches: a timer; a spotter who watches the lines, cones, and drill mechanics; and a recorder
- Most recent profile

Procedure

- Place three cones in a straight line 5 yards away from each other from the outside edges of the cones (figure 2.11). Using a reference point on the field such as the hash marks will help you run a straight line.

- Begin with one hand on the yard line. When your hand moves, the timer starts the stopwatch.

- Run to the right or left (your preference) 5 yards and touch the line with the corresponding hand. When traveling to the right, touch the yard line with your right hand. When traveling to the left, touch the yard line with your left hand. Try to stay low and not reach a full upright sprint position.

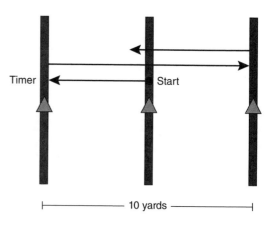

Figure 2.11   Setup for the Pro Agility.

- Run 10 yards to the third cone and touch the yard line with your hand while still facing the timer. You must never turn your back to the timer. If you do not touch the yard line with your hand, you will have to repeat the test.
- Run through the first cone from which you started. The coach stops the stopwatch when your hip crosses the starting line.
- Attempt two runs of the Pro Agility. The coach records both scores.

Three-Cone

Equipment

- Stopwatch
- Duct tape
- Three cones
- Two chairs
- Two coaches: one timer and one spotter who watches the lines, cones, and drill mechanics
- Most recent profile

Procedure

- Place three cones in an L-shape with 5 yards between the cones (figure 2.12).
- Begin in a three-point stance behind the line at the first cone. When you move your hand, the timer starts the stopwatch.
- Run to the second cone and touch the line with your right hand. Return to the first cone and touch the line with your right hand.
- Run past the second cone to the third cone and circle around the third cone and back around the second cone; then run through the line at the first cone. The timer stops the stopwatch when your hip crosses the starting line. If a cone is knocked down or your hand touches the ground after the two initial touches at the start, you are disqualified and retested.
- Attempt two runs; the coach records both attempts.

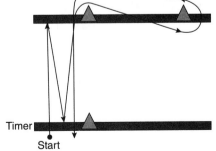

Figure 2.12   Setup for Three-Cone test.

ANAEROBIC CONDITIONING

110 Test

Equipment

- Stopwatches
- Whistle
- Cones
- Two coaches, who both act as timers on each end line

Procedure

- Set up cones along both side-lines on each end line, goal line, and 50-yard line as well as down the center of the field (figure 2.13).

- Run 110 yards 16 times. Begin in a three-point stance behind the end line.

- Make sure both coaches are ready before you start. When the coaches are ready, one blows the whistle and the coaches start their stopwatches.

- Sprint 110 yards through the opposite goal line in a required time limit. You must be across the line by the time coach yells out the time required for your position (table 2.3).

- Take a 45-second rest interval, regardless of whether you have completed the run within the time limit. The team can be tested together by creating three groups by position.

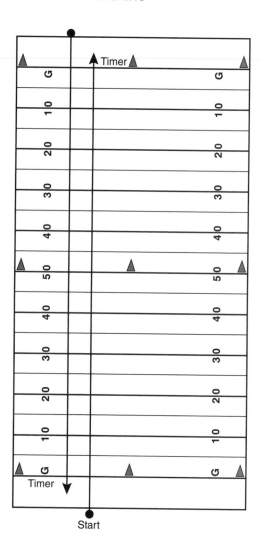

Figure 2.13 Setup for 110 Test.

Table 2.3　Suggested Times for 110 Test

Position	Suggested time
Offensive line	19 to 21 s
Defensive tackle	18 to 20 s
Defensive end, tight end, linebacker, kicker, punter	16 to 18 s
Running back, cornerback, safety, quarterback	15 to 17 s

FUNCTIONAL MOVEMENT SCREENING

The functional movement screening is used to determine each athlete's weaknesses. Weaknesses are determined by the strength and conditioning coach after he observes specific movements. The strength coach then attempts to correct any weaknesses with corrective exercises. For more on functional movement screening, refer to the FMS created by Gray Cook. (See functionalmovement.com.)

PERSONAL RECORD (PR) BOARDS

In every position coach's meeting room, there are PR boards for the position that coach oversees. Whenever a football player achieves a PR, he goes to his position coach's meeting room and erases his old PR and writes in his new one.

A well-balanced program contains some degree of testing and evaluation. Without markers for improvement, advancing a program to continue to get results is difficult. All test results should be used to evaluate the program and those participating in the program. Coaches should minimize the emphasis in any one area, and focus on individual areas of improvement and the hard work and effort of the entire team.

To get the best results from testing, coaches should incorporate a tapering period, reducing the volume of work as testing time approaches. It is best to begin with the end in mind; that is, to set the testing calendar first (table 2.4) and then plan the training calendar accordingly. Coaches should create a great environment in which to train, always find the positive, and give great effort. They should also emphasize the PR as discussed in chapter 1. When everyone competes with himself and each other, something special results. Finally, coaches need to promote and educate about proper recovery methods as described in chapter 3 to allow athletes' bodies to repair themselves.

Table 2.4 Sample Off-Season and Summer Ball Testing Schedules

Sun.	Mon.	Tues.	Wed.	Thurs.	Fri.	Sat.
Off-season testing						
	Back Squat		225 Reps Flexibility (freshmen) Body composition sign-up		Hang Clean (levels one and two) Pull-Up Flexibility (morning group only)	
					Performance testing 12:30 to 2:30 (see page 22)	
	Height Weight Picture Hang Clean (levels three and four) Flexibility (all remaining)		Bench Press		Retests	
					Performance testing 12:30 to 2:30	
Summer ball testing						
				Vertical Jump Broad Jump 225 Reps (practice) Body composition sign-up	Back Squat Body composition picture Scheduled body composition testing	
	Weight Bench Press Flexibility (newcomers) Scheduled body composition testing	FMS (newcomers) Hang Clean Flexibility Scheduled body composition testing		Pro Agility Three-Cone Pull-Up FMS	FMS 225 Reps	110 Test (all)

Chapter 3

Nutrition and Recovery

A sound nutrition program and adequate recovery are just as important, possibly more important, than any training or exercise program. Lifting, running, practice, and football games damage the body, and the only way to reverse the effects is through proper recovery and nutrition. Regardless of how hard or long you work out to get bigger, stronger, and faster, improvements will not happen unless the ongoing damage is repaired. This chapter explains methods to help with this process. The more you can do to help yourself recover, the more gains you can make, which ultimately helps the team.

EFFECTIVE SPORT NUTRITION

Proper nutrition is essential for physical development and athletic performance. Consider the physical demands placed on you by practice; competition; strength, speed, agility, plyometric, and conditioning training; and your rigorous schedule. Healthy eating habits play a valuable role in your pursuit of excellent performance.

Coaches are responsible for providing athletes with the support they require to be successful. A good coach provides the education, assessment, and support necessary to reshape nutritional habits. A coach who promotes the use of convenient, healthy snacks, recovery foods, and vitamin and mineral supplements, and who requires water bottles for every athlete demonstrates a commitment to the development of optimal nutrition habits. This support makes it possible for players to achieve a lifestyle that includes proper nutrition choices.

Performance nutrition education focuses on three primary goals: proper meal planning, balance and variety in food choices, and positive eating habits.

1. Learn proper meal planning and nutrient timing to improve your preparation and performance. Every day, eat breakfast within one hour of waking up. Eat small, frequent meals throughout the day, ideally five or six; try to eat every three to four hours. Drink water throughout the day—with every meal, before bed, and when you wake up. Make pre- and postworkout nutrition a priority.

2. Incorporate balance and variety with each meal to ensure healthy food choices. Choose meals composed of more carbohydrate than protein and more protein than fat. Substitute calorie-dense carbohydrate sources such as bread with nutrient-dense choices such as fruits and vegetables. Eat a variety of colors. Limit obviously poor choices such as fried foods, salad dressings and sauces, soft drinks, sweets, and alcohol.

3. Avoid extreme eating to promote positive eating habits and optimal food choices. Dieting doesn't work, and fads don't last. Carbohydrate is essential to supply energy for training and recovery, and everyone's diet should include some fat.

KEYS TO A PERFORMANCE-BASED DIET

- A performance-based diet is unlike other diets because it is for athletes.
- There are no fast or easy results and no money-back guarantee.
- Athletes need to make a genuine, self-motivated commitment to change their eating habits.
- Consistent healthy choices are small steps on the ladder to success.

Carbohydrate, Protein, and Fat

At its simplest, **carbohydrate** is potential energy. It is the body's preferred fuel source for basic functions and intense training. Carbohydrate, both simple and complex, provides four calories per gram and should supply the majority of your total calories each day. Your energy and performance levels will vary depending on the amount of carbohydrate, fiber, and fat you consume.

At its simplest, **protein** aids in muscle development. Muscle is constructed from individual amino acids that unite to form one functional unit or fiber that combines with other fibers to form an individual strand of muscle. Protein can supply energy when carbohydrate or fat is not available, but it is the last-resort fuel for your body. Protein provides four calories per gram. Adequate and timely protein intake is critical to the recovery process after training, especially strength training.

At its simplest, **fat** is stored energy. Fat is the largest and most efficient fuel source available to your body. It is an essential nutrient in your diet and also helps to provide a feeling of satisfaction after a meal. As a reserve supply, and a complement to carbohydrate, fat provides nine calories per gram. Your body will strive to protect a specific amount of fat stores based on your particular genetic makeup.

Top 25 Food Choices in a Performance-Based Diet

1. **Water.** Water is the single most essential component of a performance-based diet. It makes up 80 percent of your body and accounts for 65 percent of your weight.

2. **Beans.** Top-ranked carbohydrate sources such as green, black, kidney, lima, and pinto beans provide protein, fiber, and minerals essential to overall metabolism.

3. **Poultry.** Top-ranked protein sources such as baked, roasted, or grilled skinless chicken and turkey breasts contribute an excellent portion of protein with an unmatched protein-to-fat ratio.

4. **Green leafy vegetables.** Carbohydrate sources such as broccoli and spinach and leafless green, red, and yellow peppers have antioxidants, vitamins, and minerals and also deliver significant amounts of fiber.

5. **Citrus fruits and juices.** Carbohydrate sources such as oranges, grapefruit, and tangerines supply the antioxidant vitamin C, potassium, and fiber and are easily carried as wholesome snacks.

6. **Grilled or baked fish.** Fish such as salmon, tuna, sardines, and herring deliver significant amounts of protein and essential omega-3 fatty acids. These can be found in prepackaged selections.

7. **Bananas.** This carbohydrate is an excellent source of potassium and fiber with very little fat contribution and comes naturally wrapped for easy storage and transport as a wholesome snack.

8. **Nonfat dairy products.** Dairy products such as skim milk and yogurt deliver a solid protein-to-fat ratio and are an excellent source of calcium for strong bones.

9. **Berries.** Carbohydrate choices such as strawberries, blueberries, blackberries, and raspberries provide solid amounts of antioxidants (specifically, vitamin C) and potassium with no fat content.

10. **Whole grains.** Carbohydrate sources such as cereals and oatmeal and whole grain rice, bagels, and sandwich breads such as wheat or rye provide excellent amounts of fiber, iron, folic acid, and zinc.

11. **Lean beef.** Meats such as flank sirloin and filet steak plus roast beef and lean ground beef supply a good protein-to-fat ratio, B-complex vitamins, and iron.

12. **Sweet potatoes.** This carbohydrate is more of a vegetable than a starch. It contributes more protein, vitamins, and minerals than a regular potato.

13. **Sport drinks.** Electrolyte-replacement drinks quickly replenish lost water and muscle glycogen stores.

14. **Tomatoes and tomato sauce.** Carbohydrate in the form of tomatoes or tomato sauce can be included in salads, pizza, or pasta sauce, or taken as a drink. Tomatoes deliver solid amounts of potassium, fiber, vitamin C, carotenes, and lycopene, which can provide a powerful defense against several forms of cancer.

15. **Nuts.** Peanuts, almonds, walnuts, and pecans supply a solid amount of protein with essential fatty acids and the antioxidant vitamin E. Nuts are a wholesome and mobile snack.

16. **Fleshy fruits.** Carbohydrate selections such as apples, grapes, peaches, and plums supply a good amount of fiber and significant contributions of water but fewer vitamins and minerals than fruits such as citrus fruits, bananas, and berries.

17. **Eggs.** Eggs deliver a solid protein-to-fat ratio with essential fatty acids.

18. **Starchy vegetables.** Carbohydrate sources such as peas, carrots, corn, squash, cauliflower, cabbage, Brussels sprouts, and potatoes provide a good source of fiber and essential vitamins and minerals.

19. **Low-fat dairy products.** Foods such as 2 percent milk, reduced-fat cheeses, and regular yogurt supply a good protein-to-fat ratio while providing an excellent source of calcium.

20. **Recovery shakes.** This carbohydrate source provides an optimal ratio of carbohydrate to protein to ensure muscle protein and glycogen resynthesis. Recovery shakes are an affordable and transportable meal supplement or replacement.

21. **Lean pork and ham.** These choices provide a solid protein-to-fat ratio if trimmed and prepared either baked or grilled rather than fried.

22. **Dried fruit.** Dried fruit is a carbohydrate source that is longer lasting and more easily transported than fresh berries, bananas, or fleshy fruits. However, fruit loses some vitamins and minerals in the drying process.

23. **Peanut butter.** Peanut butter has a solid protein-to-fat ratio and no cholesterol. It is inexpensive and ready to eat and is an excellent complement to many of the other top 25 choices.

24. **Grains.** Carbohydrate in the form of pasta, tortillas, pita bread, cornbread, whole grain crackers, and popcorn provide good sources of fiber, iron, zinc, and folic acid.

25. **Olive oil.** As the only fat source to make the top 25 food choices, olive oil is the healthiest fat source. It is an excellent substitution for heavier, more saturated salad dressings and cooking oils.

Supplements

Supplementation can help you in your quest for optimal physical and mental development by enhancing and maintaining your energy levels throughout the day. Supplements should be taken only to complement a balanced, well-planned diet. Many nutritional supplements are safe and effective for pursuing athletic achievements. If the goal is to optimize performance through an improved body composition (i.e., developing and maintaining lean muscle while reducing percent body fat), then supplementation to ensure proper physical function is most essential. Energy bars, snacks, and drinks can be easily carried and consumed between classes, meals, practices, competitions, and tournaments, or even as evening snacks.

Before you use any supplement, you should ask yourself whether it is SAFE.

Supposed benefits. What claims of aiding training and performance are being made? Is this the best option?

Acceptable. Is it legal? Is it banned by the governing body of your sport? What side effects or risks are associated with this product?

Funding. Who is paying for it? Is it worth the money? Will you be able to afford it consistently?

Effective. Does scientific research and evidence support the supposed benefits?

When deciding which supplements to use, research the information from scientific literature published by organizations such as the International Society of Sports Nutrition (ISSN), American Dietetic Association (ADA), American College of Sports Medicine (ACSM), National Strength and Conditioning Association (NSCA), Gatorade Sports Science Institute (GSSI), and Collegiate and Professional Sports Dietetics Association (CPSDA).

Discuss your interests, questions, and concerns with a certified sport nutritionist or sport dietician. Gather your information from trusted people who are educated and informed and have a genuine commitment to your best interests.

Nutrition and Focus

Carbohydrate is the only energy source the brain can use. Because your brain cannot store carbohydrate, the fuel must come from food intake. If you are not eating enough or skipping meals, your body will start to break itself down to feed your brain. Because your brain uses twice as much energy as other cells do, concentrating, memorizing, thinking, and reacting quickly will burn up your energy supply fast.

Metabolically, the human brain is very active and uses about 20 to 30 percent of a person's energy intake at rest. Football players who do not consume adequate calories from quality food will experience decreased mental functioning.

Hydration and Focus

It takes only a 3 percent loss of body weight to negatively affect athletic performance. The effects of dehydration are immediate but can easily be reversed by drinking water.

Some of the negative effects of not drinking enough water are increased heart rate, reduced cardiac output (the amount of blood your heart can pump out at one time), decreased muscular endurance, increased core body temperature (which makes your body work harder and fatigue easier), muscle cramping, decreased balance, reduced strength and power, an inability to focus and learn new information, heat exhaustion, and heat stroke.

The brain is 80 percent water. Someone who is not hydrated cannot perform well in anything beyond basic functioning. The brain is the number-one recipient of hydration and fueling. By the time you feel thirsty, you have already lost up to 1 percent of your body weight in fluid.

Meals for Recovery

What you eat after practice or competition is as important as what you eat before and during practice or competition. Replacing fluids, carbohydrate, and protein postworkout is essential. The optimal time for carbohydrate replacement is within 30 minutes postworkout. Consuming protein in the postworkout snack assists the body with muscle repairs.

The day after a game or competition, many athletes feel tired, sore, and stiff. What they don't know is that by eating better they can minimize those feelings and recover faster. When you work out every day, sometimes twice a day, you need to choose foods that will prevent chronic fatigue and help you perform at your highest level throughout the season.

Because the weight lost during exercise is almost exclusively from sweating, you must replenish body fluids for optimal functioning. The most important thing after a hard practice or competition is to replace the fluids you've lost. Ideally, you should already be 80 percent rehydrated as a result of constant fluid replacement during practice or competition. Juice is one good choice. It supplies water, carbohydrate, vitamins, and potassium. Other good choices are sport drinks; watery foods such as watermelon, grapes, and soup; and water. You can find out how much fluid you need to consume by weighing yourself before and after your workout or competition. A good measure is to consume 200 percent of what was lost. For example, if you lost 2 pounds during exercise, drink 64 ounces of fluids (1 pound of weight = 16 ounces of fluid) to rehydrate.

In your sweat, you lose potassium, sodium, and water. Replacing the sodium is vital since it regulates your thirst. When you drink a lot of water, the sodium is diluted and your thirst goes away. Water also keeps your blood volume high, which is important in sustaining athletic performance. You can easily replenish body fluids by consuming the right foods after working out. A good option is an 8-ounce glass of orange juice for potassium and a handful of salty pretzels for sodium. Conditioning or practicing in hot conditions may make you crave salty foods as well. This is your body's way of telling you it needs some sodium. Pay attention to your body.

Previously, we discussed the 30-minute window after working out that is the optimal time to consume carbohydrate to replenish glycogen stores. During this time, the enzymes responsible for making glycogen are most active and will replace the exhausted glycogen stores at the fastest rate. Not replacing these much-needed stores can lead to overtraining. Aim for 50 grams of carbohydrate (50 x 4 grams = 200 calories) and 20 grams of protein postworkout. Two hours after that, eat a balanced meal that contains protein, starch, fruits, and vegetables. Remember that this is how much your body will naturally want, but you may be hungry for more than this. That's OK, but you will not recover any faster by eating more. Lastly, it doesn't matter whether you take in a liquid or solid form of carbohydrate. Your best choices are whole foods such as a medium bagel and orange juice or a bowl of cornflakes with milk and a banana.

Mixing a little protein with carbohydrate after working out is also a good idea. Recent research shows that this combination may be more beneficial than consuming carbohydrate alone because of the body's increased ability to rapidly restore glycogen stores using this mixture. Protein also stimulates insulin release, which helps bring glucose to the cells. The amino acids from the protein may help in the process of building and repairing muscles.

Some believe they need to take extra vitamins to replace what they lose during workouts. Be cautious when taking vitamins, and follow the directions to receive the maximum benefit. Vitamins will not help you repair damage done to your body during intense workouts. If you eat well-balanced and healthy meals, your body will naturally adjust to your training. Vitamins help to supplement your diet when you do not consume enough of the right foods.

RECOVERY

Although most aspects of improving athleticism revolve around training, the most important and most often neglected part is recovery. Without proper recovery from training, the body will not be able to repair itself.

Training without proper recovery will eventually lead to overtraining. There are many recovery methods, and each should be considered to maximize the training in any program.

Sleep

Sleep is the first step to recovery. Three major athletic areas are affected when you don't get enough sleep:

1. Cardiorespiratory performance. Sleep deprivation can reduce your cardiorespiratory performance, which will affect your performance during practice and competition and your ability to recover.

2. Information processing. As you sleep, your brain sorts all the information absorbed throughout the day. If you are not getting enough sleep, you may feel physically fine but not be able to remember the information you learned in practice or class the previous day.

3. Emotions. A lack of sleep affects emotional stability. You will become easily irritated and will not be at your peak mental state.

Other problems resulting from sleep deprivation include impaired motor functions such as delayed visual reaction time, delayed auditory response, and reduced information processing speed.

Napping is extremely important for recovering and preventing injury or illness. The ideal nap length is 20 to 30 minutes. Get the amount that works for you. If you are trying to lose weight, sleep is even more important. Certain hormones that signal fullness and hunger get confused if you don't get enough sleep.

Hydrotherapy

Hydrotherapy is the use of water to revitalize, maintain, and restore health. Immersion in water creates pressure differences that take the stress off joints during active recovery. The effect of the water pressure on the body also promotes increased blood flow for the removal of metabolic waste and the improved delivery of nutrients in the blood. A minimum time of 10 minutes will be needed to illicit any effects. Normal swimming or a pool workout may be used as a form of active recovery. Hot and cold water therapy is also useful. Cold water will be around 55 degrees Fahrenheit. Hot water will be 95 to 105 degrees Fahrenheit. Another way to use water immersion is through contrast baths—both hot and cold baths in the same session. The best use of this type of recovery is a three-to-one hot-to-cold ratio (e.g., 30 seconds cold followed by 90 seconds hot).

Massage

Sport massage facilitates recovery through biomechanical, neurological, physiological, and psychological effects. The biomechanical effects of massage are the release of soft tissue adhesions and greater joint range of motion. Neurologically, massage decreases muscle tension or spasm as well as perceived pain. The physiological effects are increased blood flow, which helps rid the body of metabolic by-products, and decreases in stress hormones, which if left unchecked impair recovery greatly. Massage also decreases feelings of anxiety and improves mood through relaxation.

Foam Roller

A foam roller can be used in place of or in conjunction with massage. Foam rolling is an inexpensive way to receive many of the same benefits as massage. One advantage of foam rolling is transportability. A foam roller can be taken anywhere—on the road, to practice, to games, or to weightlifting and conditioning sessions—or you can use it at home. Many styles, sizes, and densities are available that can be used for myofacial release and improved blood circulation.

Massage Stick

A massage stick performs the same function as a foam roller but can be used to target smaller areas. A foam roller offers more of a broad stroke; a massage stick is more exact. Just as with the foam roller, a massage stick improves flexibility, recovery, and performance while reducing the chance for injury. A massage stick can help to eliminate muscle pain and soreness and reduce the chances of repetitive strain injuries.

Chiropractic

Chiropractic therapy addresses the issues of the musculoskeletal system, especially the spine. The main focus of chiropractic therapy is adjustments to the spine, other joints, and soft tissue. It assists with posture realignment, which is critical to athletic performance. Realignment is especially essential in a collision sport such as football. Correct body alignment allows for proper mechanical functioning. Seek out a well-qualified chiropractor who has a sport background.

Physical Therapy

A physical therapist evaluates problems or difficulties by taking a history of the problem and then performing tests and measures to assess the problem. These tests include muscle strength tests, observation and movement analysis, sensory and neurological tests, flexibility tests, coordination tests, balance tests, palpation, joint motion tests, postural screening, and special tests designed for a particular problem. The physical therapist also evaluates clients' past medical histories. Physical therapy is a hands-on technique, like massage and joint mobilization, to restore joint motion or increase soft tissue flexibility.

THE FASTER PLAN

FASTER is an acronym for a specific nutrition and recovery plan that will help you as an athlete:

F—Fill up with fruits and vegetables.
A—Always hydrate.
S—Start with breakfast.
T—Think lean protein.
E—Eat often.
R—Rest and recover.

The F in the acronym refers to eating and filling your plate with fruits and vegetables. Fruits and vegetables are necessary because they provide essential vitamins, minerals, fiber, and carbohydrate to provide energy and help the body perform optimally. The A in the acronym refers to always hydrating. One of the quickest and easiest ways to positively affect performance is through proper hydration. If you are improperly hydrated, you are at a higher risk for heat-related illnesses, muscle strains, and cramps. The S in the acronym refers to starting every day with breakfast. Overnight your body uses up the food and nutrients ingested the previous day to repair the damage from workouts. A well-balanced breakfast is essential because it provides essential nutrients, vitamins, and minerals that the body will readily absorb and use for energy throughout the day. The T in the acronym encourages you to think about lean protein when you are considering your protein choices. Lean protein can be readily absorbed and used for recovery from strenuous workouts. The E in the acronym refers to eating often. Eating several meals a day plays a significant role in maintaining a healthy metabolism and providing readily-available energy. The R in the acronym refers to rest and recover. Proper rest and recovery ensure that you are obtaining the necessary and beneficial physiological adaptations to training.

Often, too much focus is put on the next lift, run, practice, or game, and not enough is put on preparing for the next lift, run, practice, or game. This thought process can lead to overtraining and mental fatigue. The more quickly you can recover, the better and more consistent your performances will be.

Part II

EXERCISES

Chapter 4

Warm-Up and Flexibility

A complete football training program must address preparing the body to perform the work of lifting, speed, agility, and plyometric activity. The warm-up is the piece of the program that accomplishes this. A well-designed warm-up can both improve performance and prevent injury. The warm-up is a good time to introduce new movements, as long as proper technique is always addressed.

Flexibility should be a part of all warm-up routines. Dynamic (motion) and static (no motion) flexibility drills should be included. Typically, dynamic flexibility is addressed preworkout, and more static flexibility is done postworkout. If static flexibility is incorporated into the preworkout routine, you should hold the stretches for less than 15 seconds.

WARM-UP

The warm-up is a very important element for the football player. Perform this part of your program before every weight and running workout or practice. Physiologically, the warm-up is critical for productive workouts and practice. Warming up prepares your muscles for exercise, increases your heart rate, and prepares your cardiovascular system for exercise. It also decreases the chance of muscle-related injuries as well as the severity of such injuries if they do occur. Warming up is imperative for greater flexibility, which is a must for improving quickness, agility, and speed.

We suggest that you begin your workout or practice with a dynamic warm-up and some stretching or foam rolling, depending on your workout. Incorporating aspects of the warm-up into a pregame routine will benefit your performance as well.

The dynamic warm-up can be used for several purposes:

- To promote dynamic flexibility through exaggerated range of motion (ROM) activities
- To teach basic movement technique (speed and agility)
- To set the tone for the workout to follow

The warm-up can change daily, which helps develop athleticism; the more movements you learn, the better you will be at learning more movements. Ideally warm-ups should be progressive.

All football players, regardless of experience level, perform the same warm-up. The younger players learn from more experienced players, who are good visual examples. Younger players require more attention as they learn what the older players already know. Older players can be taught to help the younger players.

One day a week, do a barefoot warm-up to strengthen the muscles of your feet and ankles thereby improving your balance and proprioception. This is a great way to work on speed mechanics year-round. The warm-up should be performed on a proper surface, such as field turf, and not on a hard court or concrete.

The types of warm-ups will vary depending on the time of year and the players' level of training. Each warm-up drill covers 20 yards. The number of lines needed for the warm-up will vary depending on the number of athletes, the facility size, and the number of coaches available. Typically, no more than 10 players to a line is ideal.

DYNAMIC MOVEMENT DRILLS

Reverse Walking Lunge

Procedure

- Begin with your feet hip-width apart.
- Step backward with one leg, bending with both knees to lower your body so the knee of your back leg is 1 inch above the ground and the thigh of your front leg is parallel to the ground (figure 4.1*a*). Use appropriate arm action and maintain an upright posture.
- Drive off the front leg and step backward with that leg (figure 4.1*b*). Repeat the lunge.

Figure 4.1 Reverse Walking Lunge.

Lateral Walking Lunge

Procedure

- Begin with your feet hip-width apart.
- Step laterally with one leg, pushing your hips back and fully extending the opposite leg until the thigh of the lead leg is parallel to the ground. Hold your arms straight out in front of your body to counterbalance your body weight (figure 4.2). Maintain a big, tall chest throughout the movement.

Figure 4.2   Lateral Walking Lunge.

- Drive off the lead leg, returning to the starting position with your feet hip-width apart. Repeat the lunge.

Tapioca

Procedure

- Begin with your body in the athletic position.
- Keep your center of gravity low, shoulders square, eyes up. Rotate your hips 180 degrees and take small, fast steps. Think of turning your hips so your belt buckle moves from end zone to end zone or sideline to sideline.
- Complete as many steps as possible within the prescribed distance. Repeat, initiating movement with the other leg and turning your hips in the opposite direction. Maintain the athletic position.

Fast Side Shuffle

Procedure

- Begin in a low athletic position with your feet wider than shoulder width and your toes pointing straight ahead.

- Quickly and rapidly move your feet laterally like a piston.
- Focus on quick feet and maximal reps. Keep your feet wider than shoulder-width distance, and maintain the athletic position for the prescribed distance.

Slow Side Shuffle

Procedure

- Begin in the athletic position with your feet wider than shoulder width and your toes pointing straight ahead.
- Take a small lateral step with the lead leg, pushing your hips back and pulling with the lead leg while pushing off the trail leg. Do not drag the trail foot on the ground.
- Repeat the sequence slowly, controlling the movement while maintaining your body in the athletic position for the prescribed distance.

Front Bear Crawl

Procedure

- Get in position, facedown, hands directly underneath your shoulders and your feet on the ground, hips low, and knees slightly bent.
- Reach forward with one arm followed by the forward movement of the opposite leg.
- Repeat with the opposite arm and leg. Move slowly and under control while keeping weight on the palms of your hands for the prescribed distance.

Back Bear Crawl

Procedure

- Get in position, facedown, hands directly underneath your shoulders and your feet on the ground, hips low, and knees slightly bent.
- Reach back with one leg followed by the backward movement of the opposite arm.
- Repeat with the opposite arm and leg. Move slowly and under control while keeping weight on the palms of your hands for the prescribed distance.

Crab Walk

Procedure

- Get in position, faceup, hands directly underneath your shoulders, knees bent with feet underneath hips.
- Take a small step with one leg followed by forward movement of the opposite arm.
- Repeat with the opposite arm. Move under control for the prescribed distance.

Inchworm

Procedure

- Begin in a push-up position (figure 4.3a).
- Walk your feet forward, keeping your palms flat on the ground and your legs straight (figure 4.3b).
- Begin to lift your hips into the air until your feet reach your hands with your legs straight.
- Walk your hands forward (figure 4.3c) to a push-up position and repeat for the prescribed distance.

Figure 4.3 Inchworm.

Spiderman

Procedure

- Begin in a push-up position.
- Walk forward using the arm and leg on the same side.
- Bring your knee up toward the elbow of the arm on the same side (figure 4.4) while keeping your hips low to the ground and your back leg straight.
- Repeat using the opposite arm and leg and continue for the prescribed distance.

Figure 4.4   Spiderman.

STATIONARY DYNAMIC MOVEMENTS

Arm Circles

Procedure

- Stand in a tall posture with your feet underneath your hips.
- Move an arm in a circle, keeping the arm straight.
- Repeat with the opposite arm. Rotate the arms forward and then reverse direction.

Trunk Rolls

Procedure

- Stand with your feet wider than shoulder width and your hands on your hips.
- Keeping your back flat and chest up, complete a large circular motion with your upper body.
- Repeat, circling in the opposite direction.

Knee Up and Across

Procedure

- Stand in a tall posture with your feet underneath your hips.
- Drive your knee up and across the midline of your body while extending your opposite leg.
- Maintain a tall posture throughout the movement.
- Repeat the movement with the opposite leg.

Knee Tuck

Procedure

- Stand in a tall posture with your feet underneath your hips.
- Lift one knee and grab it with both hands.
- While maintaining an upright posture, pull up on the knee and extend through your down toe.
- Repeat with the opposite leg.

Iliotibial (IT) Band

Procedure

- Stand in a tall posture with your feet underneath your hips.
- Externally rotate your hip, lifting the knee and grabbing your ankle with both hands.
- Repeat with the opposite leg.

Sample Warm-Up Routines

Perform a stationary dynamic drill between each dynamic drill in the following routines. You may also choose to perform these warm-ups barefoot. If so, perform them on a controlled surface free of sharp objects.

Continuous Dynamic Warm-Up

1. Form Run for 20 yards
2. Form Run for 20 yards
3. High Knee (page 74) for 20 yards
4. Running Butt Kick (page 75) for 20 yards
5. Carioca (page 98) for 20 yards

6. Carioca for 20 yards

7. Fast Side Shuffle to the left for 20 yards

8. Fast Side Shuffle to the right for 20 yards

Speed Dynamic Warm-Up

1. Walking Lunge (page 146) for 20 yards

2. Reverse Walking Lunge for 20 yards

3. A-March (page 72) for 20 yards

4. A-Skip (page 72) for 20 yards

5. B-March (page 73) for 20 yards

6. B-Skip (page 73) for 20 yards

Agility Dynamic Warm-Up

1. Lateral Walking Lunge 10/10

2. Backpedal (page 98)

3. Knee Up and Across (page 60)

4. Carioca 10/10

5. Tapioca 10/10

6. Slow Side Shuffle

7. Fast Side Shuffle

All-Fours Dynamic Warm-Up

1. Front Bear Crawl

2. Back Bear Crawl

3. Crab Walk

4. Inchworm

5. Spiderman

Preworkout Routine

The preworkout routine begins with a dynamic warm-up. After the last dynamic drill, athletes jog out to a designated line. The first line turns to face the group when the second line is 5 yards away. Each subsequent line lines up 2.5 yards from each other. Once athletes are in place, they begin the static stretch.

1. Standing Hamstring

2. Hip Flexor

3. Lying Quad

4. Butterfly

5. Squat Stretch

After the static stretch, the team engages in core stabilization drills or team abs. For team abs, choose any abdominal exercise in chapter 8 to be done by all athletes. The exercise must be performed with attention to detail so all athletes complete each repetition correctly. Everyone in the group is accountable. If anyone does not complete a good repetition, everyone repeats the rep or the exercise starts over.

Finish the preworkout routine with Six-Way Neck With Manual Resistance (see chapter 8, page 171).

Postworkout Flexibility

Postworkout flexibility begins with the hurdle series described in chapter 8 (page 138). Follow the hurdle series with the Front Stepover and the Lateral Step-Through. The foam roller activities may be used to ease muscle tension and relax the muscles after a challenging workout.

FOAM ROLLER

IT Band Roller

Procedure

- Place the lateral portion of your thigh (iliotibial band) perpendicularly on top of the foam roller. If necessary, cross the opposite leg over the top of the leg on the roller so the bottom of the foot is flat on the ground to initiate rolling.
- Place your arms on the ground for additional support during rolling.
- Place the majority of your weight on the foam roller and begin rolling up and down the lateral portion of your thigh from the top of the knee to the hip.

Quad Roller

Procedure

- Begin in a prone position. Place the anterior portion of your thigh (the quadriceps) perpendicularly on top of the foam roller, crossing the opposite leg over the back and placing your arms on the ground to initiate rolling.
- Place the majority of your weight on the foam roller, and begin rolling up and down the quadriceps from the top of the knee to the hip.

Low Back Roller

Procedure

- Begin in a supine position. Place the lumbar portion of your back perpendicularly on top of the foam roller. Place both feet flat on the floor to initiate rolling, and cross your arms over your upper body.
- Place the majority of your weight on the foam roller, and begin rolling up and down the lumbar portion of your back from your tailbone to the beginning of your thoracic spine.

Glute Roller

Procedure

- Sit directly on top of the foam roller. Pull the ankle of one leg on top of the knee of the opposite leg. Place one hand on the ankle and the other on the ground to initiate rolling.
- Lean to the side of the glute of the crossed leg. Place the majority of your weight on the foam roller, and begin rolling up and down and across the glute.

In-Season Warm-Ups

For the developmental level (Gun Club), the continuous dynamic warm-up teaches proper running mechanics and change of direction (COD). Advanced players on the travel squad require more challenging speed dynamic warm-up drills to maintain proper speed mechanics.

Off-Season Warm-Ups

During winter conditioning, more challenging speed and agility dynamic warm-up drills help maintain proper speed mechanics and COD. Perform a barefoot warm-up for one training session as well as an all-fours warm-up. The all-fours warm-up places compressive force through the shoulder joint. These compressive forces promote strength and stability in the shoulder.

During spring ball, continue the challenging speed and agility dynamic warm-up drills to maintain proper speed mechanics and COD. During the summer, use all types of warm-ups.

FLEXIBILITY

Ensuring the flexibility of muscle groups and joints is an important aspect of conditioning. Good flexibility allows for freedom of movement. A tight muscle cannot react properly to stress or changes of speed. A relaxed muscle has increased circulation, which helps remove the waste products that accumulate during exercise and deliver nutrients to the muscle. This increased blood supply helps with short- and long-term muscle recovery.

Stretching techniques to increase flexibility must involve three components of the muscle: the individual muscle fibers or contractile components, the connective tissue, and the nervous system.

Static Stretching

Before stretching, you need to raise your muscle temperature so that the muscle fibers and connective tissues (soft tissues) will be more pliable. This is done through low-intensity aerobic exercise such as jogging slowly (9- to 10-minute-mile pace), riding a stationary bike for 5 to 8 minutes, or performing a dynamic warm-up, which is the best method. A dynamic warm-up takes you through a variety of low-intensity movements such as High Knee, Carioca, and Side Shuffle that are related to upcoming activities.

The principle behind warming up before stretching can be explained using the example of a sponge. When a sponge is dry, it tears. When it is wet, it becomes very soft and flexible. Warming up prepares the muscles for stretching by making them pliable. Warming up prior to stretching also helps to ease the safeguards of the nervous system, which protect the muscles from working beyond their capabilities. If your stretching technique is not sound, these safeguards will be activated and will not allow your muscle fibers to lengthen.

Postworkout Stretching

The first objective of a postworkout stretching session is to educate the nerves involved to initiate relaxation. This is achieved by using a 30-second stretch to develop a slight tension in the stretching position. At the end of the 30-second stretch, the slight tension should have disappeared and the muscle should be ready to be lengthened. Quick bursts of movement may only excite the nerves involved and do little to promote long-term flexibility. In some cases, the connective tissue of the muscle will be injured and become less flexible.

Complete a stretching routine after your workout or practice as well. This will allow your muscles to elongate and restore range of motion. Because muscle temperature is high after a workout or practice, stretching is very important. Joints and ligaments are more pliable as a result of activity. At this time, static stretching is effective and can be done with your own body weight, a partner, or the assistance of a band. During a static stretch, slowly lengthen the muscle involved for approximately 30 seconds. If too much tension is developed too soon, the safeguards of the nervous system will be activated and the benefits will be lost. When this happens, slowly back off and let your muscle relax; then proceed. The correct procedure is to develop slight tension, let it fade, and then continue to achieve a greater range of motion. Remember, a tight muscle will not become flexible if you do not follow the proper techniques. Target the hamstrings, groin, low back, hip flexors, quads, and IT band with static stretching.

At the end of the workout, finish with a set of extended squats, hurdle drills, and the foam roller series. This allows your body to go through full ranges of motion, increases mobility, and breaks up microfiber adhesions developed during exercise. After every practice, finish with a quick team stretch. Focus on the hamstrings, groin, hip flexors, IT band, and low back.

KEY POINTS FOR STRETCHING TECHNIQUE

- Elevate muscle temperature through a low-intensity dynamic warm-up or aerobic activity prior to stretching.
- Use a 30-second stretch to overcome the nervous system's safeguards and relax the muscle.
- Stretch slowly to increase range of motion. Do not bounce or create tension.
- Always stretch after daily workouts and practice.

STATIC STRETCHING

Butterfly

Procedure

- Sit on the ground with your legs straight out.
- Pull the soles of your feet into your torso and together.
- Slowly push your knees to the ground with your elbows.
- Pull yourself forward to enhance the stretch.

Hip Flexor

Procedure

- Begin in a lunge position with one knee on the ground, hands on hips.
- Push your hips forward with your hands while squeezing the glute on the rear leg.
- Maintain an erect torso by tightening your core.
- The front knee should not go past the front toe during the stretch.
- Repeat with the other leg forward.

Squat Stretch

Procedure

- Spread your feet shoulder-width apart and squat down as far as possible.
- Keep your feet flat on the ground and your upper body erect.
- With your elbows inside your knees, press outward against your legs.

Seated Trunk Twist

Procedure

- Sit on the ground with your legs straight out.
- Bend your left leg and cross it over your right with your left foot flat on the ground.
- Bend your right elbow and rest it on the outside of your left thigh just above the knee. During the stretch, use your elbow to keep this leg stationary.
- With your left hand resting behind you, slowly rotate your entire torso and look over your left shoulder.
- Repeat, switching legs and rotating in the other direction.

Lying Quad

Procedure

- Lie on your side and rest your head in the palm of your hand.
- Grasp your upper foot and pull the heel to the buttocks to stretch the quadriceps. During the stretch, squeeze your glutes.

- Maintain a straight line from head to toe.
- Roll over to the other side and stretch the other quad.

Standing Hamstring

Procedure

- Stand with your legs straight and your feet together.
- Slowly push your hips back and lower your chest while reaching for your toes until you feel a stretch in your hamstrings. Do not overstretch.

YOGA AND PILATES

Yoga and Pilates help with flexibility, balance, whole body strength, efficiency, power, and body awareness. Both exercise forms focus on breathing, which improves mental focus and emotional stability. Find a qualified instructor to use this type of exercise.

FLUSHING AND REGENERATION

Flushing or regenerating protocols accelerate the healing process between training sessions. A flush workout uses a form of movement such as dynamic or static stretching as a warm-up followed by mobility and stability exercises. Exercises for lengthening muscles and correcting motor patterns may also be included. Finally, static stretching, foam rolling, and massage sticks are recommended for the completion of a flush workout.

CONCLUSION

A proper warm-up and flexibility program prepares you physiologically, psychologically, and emotionally. It also provides a chance for team building by putting the leaders in position to lead. During warm-up and flexibility time, teams can work on communication skills and chemistry. A properly designed and organized warm-up can provide the motivation you and your team need.

Chapter 5

Speed

There are many components of speed development for football. The five main factors that can improve speed are as follows:

- Developing overall strength
- Increasing the rate of force development
- Increasing stride frequency
- Increasing stride length
- Improving running form

When training to improve these speed components, you must emphasize total development in the legs, abdominals, and low back. Strengthening these muscle groups is paramount. Along with added muscle strength, these groups also need added flexibility. Finally, these groups must be conditioned to withstand the intense load sprinting will put on them. A stronger, more flexible, better-conditioned muscle will increase overall speed and performance.

Improving stride frequency and improving running form are also important and specific to increased performance. In few sports other than track do athletes get the opportunity to increase their stride length. Football demands movements associated with acceleration, change of direction, and quickness for success.

An effective way to increase your stride frequency is to focus on drills such as running downhill and agility-related drills that force you to accelerate and move your feet quickly.

Always use an extended warm-up and stretching routine before engaging in a strenuous speed improvement program. After the workout, take 10 to 15 minutes to cool down and stretch. This is the most important time to stretch because the muscles are warm and most elastic.

SPEED IMPROVEMENT VOCABULARY

It is important to have a vocabulary when working on speed technique. This ensures that the message is the same regardless of which coach or trainer corrects an athlete. The athletes will understand quickly what is being addressed. A common vocabulary also allows more athletes to be coached in a team setting. The vocabulary described in this section was developed by Kevin McNair.

Upper-Body Terms

- **Focus:** Eyes straight ahead at a conversational level as if you were talking to someone your own height. Pick a point off into the distance at the same height as your eyes and stare at it.

- **Hand position:** Hands facing torso with fingers curled and the thumb on the forefinger. It is important to have your hands relaxed and not clenched.

- **Fix:** This is in reference to the angle of the elbow. Fix a 90-degree angle in the elbow joint and do not let it change during the arm action. Do not let the arm straighten out at the bottom or bend too much at the top.

- **Rotate:** Move the arms through a full range of motion. The rotation occurs through the shoulders. Imagine an axis running through one shoulder and out the other, and the shoulders rotating as wheels. The shoulders remain relaxed during running. Shrugging the shoulders creates tension down the chain and impairs speed. With elbows fixed, the knuckles move down, not back, through the pocket past the glutes with an explosive downward force. The range of motion begins at the chest, no higher than the sternum.

- **Squeeze:** Anytime the elbows move too far away from the midline, you produce a rotational force. You must concentrate on getting your elbows tight against your body. To accentuate speed, you must have everything moving in a linear fashion.

- **Hammer:** The arm movement downward should be a violent motion. The knuckles must be in a down and back position with palms facing in as though you were standing with your back to a wall hammering a nail into the wall.

Lower-Body Terms

- **Arch:** There should be a slight arch in the low back. Bring the shoulder blades (scapulae) of the upper back slightly toward the midline of the body by squeezing them together. Maintain a slight angular body lean. Do not bend at the waist. Keep the core as rigid as possible.

- **Punch:** Punch the knee forward with the ankle dorsiflexed.
- **Foot plant:** The foreleg snaps down and the foot strikes slightly behind the hips, not directly underneath. The foot will naturally hit on the ball of the foot.
- **Extension:** Lock out the plant leg to triple extension. If you come out of this phase too early, you will not maximize your stride length and power.

The drills in this chapter will help you become more technically proficient. If the work is to be done in a group setting, the drills are set up in the following order. Not all drills will be done from the beginning. As you become proficient, you will perform more drills.

SPEED DEVELOPMENT

Seated Arm Action

Purpose

- Focus, hand position, fix

Procedure

- Sit with upright posture with your legs outstretched in front of your body.
- Relax your arms and keep your elbows flexed at a 90-degree angle during the entire range of motion. The shoulder joint is the pivot point in this movement.
- Your hand comes to chin height at the top of the movement with your thumb pointed up.
- Your palm turns out slightly so that your thumb brushes your hip on the downward movement.
- Your arms must not cross the center line of your torso and must stay in the line with your shoulder.

Coaching Points

- Work these techniques in a slow, smooth fashion at first. Do not try to go too fast and compromise technique.
- Progress from 50 percent to 100 percent (full speed) at 10 percent increments.

Standing Arm Action

Purpose

- Focus, hand position, fix, rotate

Procedure

- Stand with a slight bend at the waist.
- Properly swing your arms alternately as was done in the Seated Arm Action.
- A partner may stand in front of you with his hands as high as your chin. Your knuckle will touch your partner's hands with each upward swing of your arm.
- Shoulders are relaxed and elbows are fixed at a 90-degree angle during the entire range of motion. The shoulder joint is the pivot point in this movement.
- The palm will turn out slightly so that the thumb brushes the hip on the downward movement.
- Arms must not cross the center line of the torso and must stay in the line with the shoulder.

Coaching Points

- Work on these techniques in a slow, smooth fashion at first. Do not compromise technique or try to go too fast.
- The partner must keep his hands at the level of your chin.
- Progress from 50 percent to 100 percent (full speed) at 10 percent increments.

A-March/A-Skip

Purpose

- A-March: all upper body
- A-Skip: arch, punch, extension

Procedure

- Marching is defined by a pause after each repetition. Skipping is performed continuously.
- Maintain proper arm action as with sprinting. Keep your center of gravity over the ball of your foot.

- Raise your knee to at least waist level with your ankle dorsiflexed and above the opposite knee. Do not bend at the waist to achieve knee height.
- The plant leg should be fully extended at the ankle, knee, and hip.
- During the descent, drive the leg down forcefully to claw the ground under the body's center of gravity.

Coaching Points

- Cycle the legs through in a rhythmic fashion.
- Emphasize a quick leg response when contracting the ground. Claw the ground.
- Maintain proper arm action.

B-March/B-Skip

Purpose

- B-March: all upper body, foot plant
- B-Skip: arch, punch, foot plant, extension

Procedure

- Marching is defined by a pause after each repetition. Skipping is performed continuously.
- Use the same technique as in the A-Skip. However, at the top of the leg cycle, the knee simultaneously is extended and the leg pulled down forcefully to claw the ground under the body's center of gravity.
- Your foot should strike the ground slightly behind your hip.
- Keep your center of gravity over the ball of your foot.
- All lower-body movements should coordinate with upper-body and arm actions.

Coaching Points

- At the top of the leg cycle, extend your knee fully and maintain your rhythm.
- Emphasize a quick leg response when contacting the ground. Claw the ground.
- Maintain proper arm action.

High Knee

Purpose

- All upper body, arch, punch, extension

Procedure

- Using the basic fundamentals of sprinting, drive your knee upward while moving forward. Pick up speed as you move forward.
- When your knee is in the up position, your thigh should be at least parallel to the ground with your foot above the opposite knee (figure 5.1). Your ankle is dorsiflexed. Your upper body should be tall with your low back arched and rigid for support.
- Your center of gravity should be over the ball of your foot.

Figure 5.1   High Knee.

Coaching Points

- Keep your head and eyes up.
- Emphasize repetitions, coordination, and rhythm in the upper and lower body.
- Emphasize technique and repetition, not speed.

Running Butt Kick

Purpose

- All upper body, arch, extension

Procedure

- Using the basic fundamentals of sprinting, now pull your heels to your butt (figure 5.2) while moving forward. Pick up speed as you move forward.
- The emphasis is on contracting the hamstring quickly while performing maximum repetitions over the prescribed distance.
- Your upper body should be tall with your low back arched and rigid for support.
- Your center of gravity should be over the ball of your foot.
- There should be a coordinated movement with the lower body and the arm action producing a bouncing effect.

Figure 5.2   Running Butt Kick.

Coaching Points

- Keep your head and eyes up.
- Emphasize repetitions, coordination, and rhythm in the upper and lower body.
- Emphasize technique and repetitions, not speed, by progressing from 50 percent to 100 percent (full speed) at 10 percent increments.

Fast Leg

Purpose

- Arch, punch, extension, foot plant

Procedure

- Begin with short, quick steps. On every third step, perform a full leg cycle with the appropriate arm action. This must be done explosively.
- Maintain dorsiflexion and pull your leg down quickly to the ground.
- Take three short steps between fast leg actions.
- Work with one leg for the designated distance.

Coaching Points

- Keep your torso in an upright position with your low back rigid for support. Do not bend at the waist to get needed knee drive.
- Emphasize cycling the leg through the range of motion as quickly as possible.
- Gather yourself and stay balanced by taking small steps before performing the next repetition.

Dead Leg

Purpose

- Arch, punch, extension, foot plant

Procedure

- Begin with short, quick steps. With every step, perform a full leg cycle with the appropriate arm action. This must be done explosively.
- Keep your toe up and pull your leg down quickly to the ground.
- Keep the noncycling leg dead (stable) by squeezing the quad and bouncing on the ball of the foot. Make sure this leg travels in a straight line and does not swing laterally.
- Work with one leg for the designated distance.

Coaching Points

- Keep your torso in an upright position with your core rigid for support.
- Emphasize cycling the leg through the range of motion as quickly as possible.

Backward Run

Purpose

- Extension

Procedure

- Your body should be in a position that would look like the stride if done in reverse.
- Maintain your center of gravity over the ball of your foot.
- Flex your heel to your butt.
- Extend your leg straight back almost parallel to the ground.
- Land on the ball of your foot.

Coaching Points

- Keep your head and eyes up.
- Emphasize technique and repetition, not speed.

C-Skip

Purpose

- Hammer, arch, punch, extension
- This is a medium-level plyometric exercise.

Procedure

- Use the same technique as in the A-Skip variations. However, the emphasis of this variation is height or distance.
- Drive your knee as high as possible and explode off the plant leg with full extension to get maximum height or distance.
- Use your arms to propel your body up.
- Maintain your center of gravity over your toes.
- All lower-body movements should coordinate with upper-body and arm actions.

Coaching Points

- Use the same mechanics as with all the A-Skip variations, but emphasize height or distance.
- Exaggerate the arm action to achieve maximum elevation.
- Focus on maximum explosion off the single leg.

Bounding

Purpose

- Punch, extension, foot plant
- This is a high-level plyometric exercise.

Procedure

- Explode off one leg and reach to cover as much ground as possible and land on the opposite foot.
- Drive with your knee and do not reach with your foot.
- This movement will look somewhat like an exaggerated stride.

Coaching Points

- Keep your head and eyes up.
- Maintain proper arm action.
- Try to cover as much ground as possible.
- Emphasize technique and height and distance, not speed.

Single-Leg Hop

Purpose

- Extension, foot plant
- This is a high-level plyometric exercise.
- This drill increases explosion in the hips.

Procedure

- Explode off one leg. Try to cover as much ground as possible before you land on the same foot.
- Reach with the knee, not the foot, of the nondriving leg.

Coaching Points

- Keep your head and eyes up.
- Maintain proper arm action.
- Try to cover as much ground as possible.
- Emphasize technique and getting height and distance.
- Emphasize the cycling of the plant leg.

Form Run or Stride

Purpose

- All techniques

Procedure

- Combine all technique drills.
- Work on proper arm swing, hinging at the shoulder with a 90-degree bend at the elbow, hands moving from pockets to armpits.
- Your arms and legs should move within the framework of your body, not side to side.
- Your center of gravity should be over your toes. Keep your core rigid. Do not bend at the waist.
- Keep your shoulders back. Set your center of gravity by leaning your whole body forward.

Coaching Points

- Use proper arm action with all movements.
- Keep your head and eyes up.
- Emphasize technique and repetition, not speed.
- Stay loose and relaxed.

Scramble-Up

Purpose

- Punch, extension

Procedure

- Lie on your abdomen with your waist on the goal line.
- Quickly scramble to your feet and sprint the prescribed distance.

Coaching Point

- Explode up from the start position.

40-Yard Stance and Start

It is important to have a procedure for getting in a good, comfortable stance to allow for an explosive start.

Purpose

- Fix, rotate, hammer, punch, foot plant, extension

Equipment

- Football field or other surface marked with 5-yard increments
- Stopwatch

Procedure

- Use the goal line on the football field as the starting line.
- The timer (coach) is positioned on the 10-yard line.
- Use the call and response routine to get positioned correctly behind the starting line.

Coaching Points

- Position the line: Place your front foot 6 to 12 inches (two or three fists) away from the starting line.
- Hand position: Place one hand on your hip pocket and the other hand just below the line.
- Lead hand: Sweep back the lead hand in an explosive manner.
- Back hand: Rip the back hand forward from your pocket with a quick motion.
- Foot stagger: Stand with the toes of the back foot at the heel of the lead foot, feet hip-width apart.
- Feet: Explode with both legs. The back leg should not go too far on the first step, but you must try to get it out in front of you. Do not step to the side.
- Head: Tuck your chin to your chest, eyes looking toward feet.
- Forward lean: Before takeoff, lean forward as far as possible without losing your balance and pause for 1 second.

The Call and Response routine is used in conjunction with the McNair system. In the Call and Response routine, the coach calls a number and the players respond to the call with an answering phrase and then action.

Coach (call): "1"

Athlete (response): "Let's have some fun."

Procedure: Make two fists and stack one on the other.

Coach: "2"

Athlete: "Touch your shoe."

Procedure: Keep your fists together and place your hands directly behind the starting line and in front of your front foot. You may need to adjust depending on your particular needs. A right-handed athlete places his left foot forward; vice versa for a left-handed athlete.

Coach: "3"

Athlete: "Drop your knee."

Procedure: Drop the opposite knee right beside the front foot.

Coach: "4"

Athlete: "Hand on the floor."

Procedure: Take the hand on the side of the back foot and place the thumb and index finger right behind the line with the thumb right in front of the center of the kneecap.

Coach: "5"

Athlete: "High five."

Procedure: Take the hand on the side of the front foot and place it about a foot in front of the line for balance.

Coach: "6"

Athlete: "Hips up quick"

Procedure: As you rise, your back foot slides forward so there is a heel-to-toe relationship and balance in the stance.

Coach: "7"

Athlete: "Elbow to heaven."

Procedure: Take the balance hand in front of the line, bend your elbow 90 degrees, and place your hand right beside your hip.

Coach: "8"

Athlete: "Run straight."

Procedure: Explode low out of the stance and run straight.

40-YARD DASH

Many people question the benefits of running 40-yard dashes. With a well-designed program from warm-up to execution and good monitoring of runs, running 40s should not be any more of a risk than squatting heavy.

To get fast, you need to run fast. This means that training must be devoted to maximal or near-maximal runs. Adding 40-yard runs to a well-designed off-season program will improve both speed and confidence.

HIGH- AND LOW-INTENSITY RUNS

Running may be broken down into high, medium, and low intensity. To improve football speed, you need to perform primarily high- and low-intensity runs. High-intensity runs are at 95 percent maximum speed or more. Low-intensity runs are at 75 percent maximum speed or less. High-intensity runs stimulate the nervous system sufficiently to increase speed. Low-intensity runs improve muscular capacity by increasing the capillary and mitochondrial density of the muscle and its ability to perform prolonged work and recover (speed endurance).

A minimum of 48 hours is necessary for recovering from high-intensity work because of the demands on the central nervous system (CNS). Therefore, you should perform low-intensity runs between high-intensity sessions.

This is a typical sequence for a four-day workout split:

Monday: Low

Tuesday: High

Thursday: Low

Friday: High

Note: Training in the weight room and training on the field are not mutually exclusive. If you are going to increase the intensity of your runs, you will need to decrease the volume of lifting and vice versa. This concept will be discussed in greater detail in chapters 10 through 12.

SPEED DRILLS

Downhill Run

Purpose

- Arch, punch, foot plant

Equipment

- Grassy hill with an approximately 3 to 6 percent grade downhill (excessive decline will result in deceleration)
- Cones

Procedure

- Place starting and finishing cones 20 to 30 yards apart.
- Start with your hand or foot behind the cone.
- Run from the starting cone to the finishing cone.

Coaching Points

- Keep your torso upright and your core rigid for support.
- Make sure to decelerate properly. Lower your center of gravity by dropping your hips and bending your knees.

Uphill Run

Purpose

- Extension, punch, fix, rotate

Equipment

- Grassy hill with an approximately 10 to 30 percent grade uphill (excessive incline will result in form alteration)
- Cones

Procedure

- Place starting and finishing cones 15 to 25 yards apart.
- Start with your hand or foot behind the cone.
- Run from the starting cone to the finishing cone.

Coaching Points

- Keep your torso upright and your core rigid for support.
- Use proper arm action with all movements.

Stadium Stair Run

Purpose

- Extension, punch, fix, rotate

Equipment

- Stadium or building with stairs

Procedure

- Start at the bottom row of stairs.
- Sprint to a designated point. Covering the required distance should take 10 seconds or less.
- Walk back down the stairs to recover.

Coaching Points

- Allow enough rest to give full effort to develop speed.
- Emphasize fast turnover with the feet.

Build-Up

Purpose

- All techniques

Equipment

- Lined football field
- Cones

Procedure

- Accelerate into a form run (stride) to 70 percent effort for 10 to 20 yards until you reach the first cone.
- Once you reach the first cone, gradually increase your effort to 80 percent over the next 10 to 20 yards until you reach the second cone.
- Once you reach the second cone, gradually increase your speed to 90 or 100 percent effort over the next 10 to 20 yards until you reach the final cone.
- Gradually decelerate properly. Lower your center of gravity by dropping your hips and bending your knees.

SPEED GROUPS

Initially, the team is divided into 10 groups based on 40-Yard Dash times. Throughout the summer, groups compete in different events such as Shuttle, Backpedal, and Scramble-Up, and each player tries to move up to faster groups.

Automatic demotion occurs if you do any of the following:

- Talk back to a coach
- Complain in general
- Display an overall negative attitude (e.g., by not competing)
- Are assessed penalties (e.g., offside or false starts)

Winning in your group earns you a promotion to the next highest group. Winning rules are determined by the strength staff depending on the event and number of reps to be run.

SUMMER BALL

During summer training, three of the four training days are used to develop the various components of speed. On Mondays, focus on speed technique (low intensity). On Tuesdays, work on lateral speed and agility (high intensity). On Fridays, focus on plyometrics and acceleration and deceleration (high intensity).

Lateral Speed

There is a difference between lateral speed and linear speed. Consider a defender who recognizes a lateral toss sweep play and turns and runs down the line of scrimmage. This is not lateral speed. An example of a display of true lateral speed is a linebacker scraping when he recognizes a zone play and has to get to the outside while keeping his shoulders square to protect against the cutback. This type of movement requires more involvement from the inner thigh muscles (adductors, gracilis, vastus medialis, etc.) and outer thigh muscles (abductors, gluteus medius, tensor fascia latae [TFL], etc.). Carioca, Side Shuffle, and High Knee Crossover at high speeds are great for developing lateral speed.

Deceleration

Speed development is crucial to your success as a football player. However, having a lot a speed will not be very beneficial unless you can control it. The ability to decelerate and stop is also a very important aspect of football performance. Deceleration occurs when the body's center of gravity moves to a position just behind where the foot will strike the ground. Proper deceleration involves keeping your hips down and low with your torso upright and your eyes focused on the target. Do not take proper deceleration mechanics for granted. They must be trained to reduce the risk of noncontact ACL injuries.

Rather than performing specific drills for deceleration, try to incorporate deceleration techniques into your regular program and drills by focusing on the mechanics of stopping and changing direction. For example, when doing sprints, go through the finish line and give yourself 10 yards to come to a complete stop and finish in an athletic position.

Acceleration

A majority of your time is spent accelerating. Rarely is top speed a factor in football. Therefore, it is important to spend time on drills that improve acceleration.

Sled Pull

Purpose

- Punch, extension, foot plant

Equipment

- Football field or similar training surface
- Sled
- Harness
- 10-foot strap
- Weight plates
- Cones

Procedure

- Place finishing cones 20 to 40 yards from the starting line.
- Use the harness and the strap to attach the weight plates to your torso.
- Start with your hand or foot behind the starting line and run past the finish line (figure 5.3).

Figure 5.3   Sled Pull.

Coaching Points

- Your center of gravity should be in front of your toes to create forward lean.
- Keep your torso upright and your core rigid for support.
- Use proper running mechanics.
- Do not use too much weight. If your running form is compromised, reduce the amount of weight on the sled.

Partner Resistance

Purpose

- Punch, extension, foot plant

Equipment

- Football field or similar training surface
- Harness
- 10-foot strap with handle
- Cones

Procedure

- Place finishing cones 10 to 30 yards from the starting line.
- Attach the harness and strap to your torso. Your partner stands behind you and stretches the strap before you start. He will move with you as you run.
- Start with your hand or foot behind the starting line and run past the finish line.
- Your training partner keeps the tension constant as you run (figure 5.4).

Figure 5.4 Partner Resistance.

Coaching Points

- Make sure the harness and strap are securely fastened.
- Use proper running mechanics.
- Do not use too much resistance. If your running form is compromised, reduce the amount of tension on the strap.

CONCLUSION

Developing speed is a year-round effort that requires proper planning. No phase or season is less important than any other because they all can be used to develop some component of speed. During the off-season and summer, emphasize developing overall strength and maximizing force production and absorption. Use spring football and the in-season to focus on improving your running technique because this is not highly taxing on the central nervous system. Increased stride length and frequency are the by-products of a system of training that addresses strength, force production and absorption, stability, mobility, balance, and flexibility.

Chapter 6

Quickness and Agility

As discussed in chapter 5, acceleration and deceleration are key components in football skill. In this chapter, we discuss the ability to decelerate, change direction, and accelerate quickly. In the sport of football, you need these skills to react and move over and around obstacles in the competitive environment. Improvements in agility parallel those of linear speed in that improvements in overall strength and the rate of force development are important factors. Agility requires a combination of balance, speed, strength, and coordination, as defined here:

- Balance is the ability to maintain your center of gravity over your base of support when stationary or moving so you don't fall over.
- Speed is stride length multiplied by stride frequency.
- Strength is the ability of a muscle or muscle group to overcome a resistance.
- Coordination is the ability to control the movement of your body in cooperation with your body's sensory functions—the eyes, ears, and proprioceptive mechanism in the joints.

Agility also requires the ability to react quickly to visual or auditory stimuli. This is often referred to as a player's quickness. Later we will discuss how to incorporate these stimuli into drills.

Agility can be classified as general or specific according to its relation to your sport or event. Further, in consideration of all possible movement patterns, agility can be classified as programmed/closed (Pro Agility, Three-Cone) or nonprogrammed/open (Mirror Drill).

Always use a proper dynamic or agility-based warm-up (see chapter 4) before engaging in a strenuous routine. After the workout, take 10 to 15 minutes to cool down and stretch. This is the most important time to stretch because the muscles are warm and most elastic.

As with any other form of training (speed, strength, etc.), in agility training you must develop proper technique. First, your eyes must always be focused directly ahead or on the visual target. Changes in direction or transitions are performed by first getting your head around and finding the appropriate point of focus. Second, just as in straight-ahead speed, the role of the arm action is vital to acceleration. Explosive arm action created by driving the elbows down and keeping a relatively fixed, 90-degree elbow position should be used when reaccelerating. Finally, you must attend to proper deceleration mechanics. Deceleration from a given velocity depends heavily on strength and the relationship between the center of gravity and the base of support. Deceleration is a skill that must be learned progressively. The athlete's ability to decelerate from various speeds and directions should be trained to reduce the risk of injury. This may be done with Build-Up drills in which you accelerate to an approximate determined speed such as 60 to 90 percent max speed, and then decelerate to a complete stop within 10 yards.

FOOTBALL AGILITY TRAINING

Programmed events such as the Three-Cone, Pro Agility, and other cone drills work lateral speed and change of direction mechanics. As with any other form of training, pay attention to developing proper technique. Following are three areas to target:

1. Getting the head around and finding the appropriate point of focus
2. Using the arm action when accelerating just as in straight-ahead speed
3. Using proper deceleration mechanics (see chapter 5)

During specific times of the year, focus on developing agility and quickness. During the winter off-season, for example, use an organized approach in which you train at stations, each of which has a specific emphasis. The team rotates through three stations: Speed, Mat Drills, and Agility. Attention to detail, focus, and mental toughness are expected at all three stations. The drills performed at the stations during this time are not new, but the organization and the attention to detail and high demand for enthusiasm from the coaches are key. Each station uses the same instructor commands, and each drill demands the same intensity, focus, and enthusiasm. An instructor is at each station, and the athletes sprint from station to station.

STATION 1: SPEED

Speed training during the off-season addresses the technical aspects of running and features select plyometric drills to develop explosiveness.

At the station, the athletes follow the coach's commands:

- Breakdown: The first two lines assume an athletic position—head up, feet shoulder-width apart, hands off thighs.
- Set: The first line quickly sets up into 40-yard start stance.
- Go: The line fires out 5 to 10 yards; then executes the drill for 20 yards.

These are the drills performed at the Speed station (see chapter 5):

- Seated Arm Action
- Standing Arm Action
- A-March
- A-Skip
- B-March
- B-Skip
- High Knee
- Running Butt Kick
- Fast Leg (Right/Left)
- Dead Leg (Right/Left
- Backward Run
- C-Skip for Height
- C-Skip for Distance
- Bounding
- Single-Leg Hop (Right/Left)
- Form Run or Stride
- Scramble-Up

STATION 2: MAT DRILLS

Mat Drills can be completed on wrestling mats or on field turf. Mark off an area 15 × 15 yards. Athletes line up three across and a minimum of 10 lines deep.

At the station, the athletes follow the coach's commands:

- Breakdown: The first two lines assume an athletic position—head up, feet shoulder-width apart, hands off thighs. After the drill is initiated and the first line has gone, this command will not be used again unless the group is starting over.
- Set: The next line quickly steps into the drill area, feet chopping (moving rapidly up and down).
- Go: The line on the mat executes the drill.
- Ready, ready: Players return to the athletic position, chopping the feet and evening out the line while waiting for the next command.
- Fire out: Players sprint across the mat, forward roll at the end of the mat, and come up chopping their feet. They sprint all the way off the mat in the direction in which the coach points. All players must be in a line and chopping their feet before the coach sends them off the mat.

Keys to Mat Drills

- Each drill is approximately six seconds long.
- Each drill must be done with great speed and quickness.
- Each drill must be done perfectly by all players on the line or the group is sent back to do it again until it is done perfectly.
- Coaches and athletes demonstrate intensity. Perfection is demanded.
- Players forward roll on tape two thirds of the way across the mat or at the 10-yard mark. After the roll, each player must come to his feet in an athletic position, chopping the feet rapidly, and get his eyes on the coach at the end of the mat for the exit direction.
- The coach sends players straight off the mat after the first drill to get warmed up. After the first drill, the coach sends players off to the right, left, or straight.
- First-year players are limited to 11 minutes (week 1), 13 minutes (week 2), and 15 to 17 minutes (week 3+). Coaches should gradually build up the time players spend at each station to allow proper adaptation and minimize the risk of injury to athletes.
- The Mat Drills end with a horn blowing, at which point players rotate to the next station.

High Knees Mat Drill

Procedure

- Drive your knees up as high as you can (figure 6.1).
- Bring your knees to your chest as rapidly as possible with your arms and knees together. (See chapter 5.)

Figure 6.1   High Knees Mat Drill.

Two-Point Shuffle Wave Mat Drill

Procedure

- Chop your feet.
- Shuffle right, left, forward, or back, whichever direction the coach points.
- Keep your eyes on the coach.

Two-Point Seat Roll Mat Drill

Procedure

- From a standing position, drop to your backside and roll over.
- Stand up, chopping your feet.

Four-Point Seat Roll Mat Drill

Procedure

- Dive out on the mat, stay on all fours, and chop your feet.
- Roll in the direction the coach points.

Four-Point Directional Wave Mat Drill

Procedure

- Dive out on the mat and start chopping your feet.
- Move in the direction the coach points—right, left, forward, back, or down—as fast as possible.

Two-Point Sprint Wave Mat Drill

Procedure

- Chop your feet.
- Sprint right, left, forward, or back, whichever direction the coach points.
- Keep your eyes on the coach.

Mirror Mat Drill

Procedure

- Before the drill begins, the coach chooses a rabbit.
- The rabbit runs to the middle of the mat.
- The other players react as the rabbit tries to lose them by quickly changing direction. The rabbit can hit the ground only once per time on the mat.

Spinning Wheel Mat Drill

Procedure

- Dive on the mat, chopping your feet.
- On the coach's command, bear crawl forward and spin on your right hand.
- Continue forward and spin on your left hand.

- Execute a forward roll and follow the coach's next command.

Quarter Eagle Mat Drill

Procedure

- While chopping your feet, open your hips in the direction the coach points (figure 6.2).
- Return to the starting position while facing the coach, feet chopping.

Figure 6.2   Quarter Eagle Mat Drill.

STATION 3: AGILITY

As a group, run to the coach to await further instructions. This station is split into two sections. The first section is up to eight minutes long and is split into three groups of programmed or nonprogrammed drills: Six-Bag Drills, Cone Drills, and Speed Ladder Drills. The second section of station 3 features a combination agility groups that last from six to nine minutes.

The coach's commands are the same as they are at the speed development station: breakdown, set, and go.

Six-Bag Drills

Equipment

- Agility bags

Procedure

- Set up six agility bags 3 yards apart (figure 6.3).
- Shuffle, backpedal, and sprint around the bags. You can substitute Carioca and Shuffle into the sprint movements.

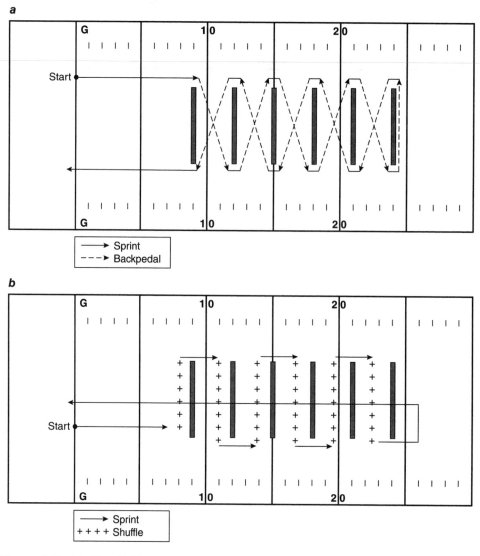

Figure 6.3   Six-Bag Drills.

Cone Drills

Procedure

- Set up four cones 10 yards apart in a square.
- **Drill 1:** Sprint from cone 1 to cone 2, carioca from cone 2 to cone 3, shuffle from cone 3 to cone 4, and then turn and run.
- **Drill 2:** Backpedal from cone 1 to cone 2, shuffle from cone 2 to cone 3, carioca from cone 3 to cone 4, and then turn and run.
- **Drill 3:** Bear crawl from cone 1 to cone 2, shuffle from cone 2 to cone 3, backpedal from cone 3 to cone 4, and then turn and run.
- Be sure to drop your hips and bend your knees as you run through each cone. If you don't, you will have to repeat the drill.

Speed Ladder Drills

Procedure

- Set up one or two speed ladders. If you use two ladders, place them 10 yards apart.
- **Drill 1:** Run through the speed ladder, putting one foot in each rung. Sprint out 5 yards.
- **Drill 2:** Run through the speed ladder, putting two feet in each rung. Sprint out 5 yards.
- **Drill 3:** Lateral shuffle through the speed ladder with one foot in each rung. Sprint out 5 yards.
- **Drill 4:** Stand beside the speed ladder. Alternate stepping in and out of each rung, one foot at a time. Sprint out 5 yards.

Combination Agilities

Combination, or combo, agilities can also be used as part of a football training program. These are a great tool to incorporate both agility and reactive (quickness) components. These drills are used mostly during the off-season summer training period. The title refers to the pairing of two or more movements that will be executed on command, either by voice or whistle. The movements are performed over a 25- to 30-yard distance.

The actual pattern is determined by the coach administering the drill. For example, Sprint–Backpedal–Sprint (SP–BP–SP) can be done in a straight line for 30 yards. The coach has the flexibility to determine the number of yards you will cover in any given drill. Creativity is the only limitation.

The number of patterns is endless:

Sprint–Backpedal–Sprint

Sprint–360–Sprint

Bear Crawl–Forward Roll–Sprint

Sprint–Stop–Sprint–Stop–Sprint

Backpedal–Sprint–Turn and Run

Sprint–Carioca–Carioca–Sprint

Bear Crawl–Forward Roll–Backpedal–Sprint

- **Backpedal:** Stay low, keeping your center of gravity over your toes, and go as fast as possible.
- **Side Shuffle:** Keep your center of gravity low and move laterally.
- **Carioca:** Keep your center of gravity low, shoulders square, eyes up. Rotate your hips 180 degrees. Think of turning your hips so your belt buckle moves from end zone to end zone or sideline to sideline.
- **360:** Run linearly. Drop your hips and rotate as fast as possible by throwing your elbows around violently and whipping your head around.
- **Forward Roll:** While moving forward, place your hands on the ground in front of you, tuck your chin, and stay in a tightly tucked position. As you uncoil, place your feet on the ground and return to an athletic position.

SPRING BALL AND IN-SEASON

As part of your practice routine during spring ball and the regular season, one to two minutes after the dynamic warm-up can include an agility period that uses the drills described in the Mat Drill section. This will help wake up your nervous system and set the tone for practice.

SUMMER BALL

During summer training, more drills are incorporated that include resistance and overspeed as well as the movements of the various positions played on the field.

Reaction, Acceleration, Change of Direction, Effort (RACE) Drills

Equipment

- Three agility bags and seven cones

Procedure

- Place the first bag 7 yards from the start line. Place the next two bags behind the first with 3 yards between bags. Place the cones according to figure 6.4.
- Sprint, backpedal, hop, and shuffle as shown in figure 6.4.

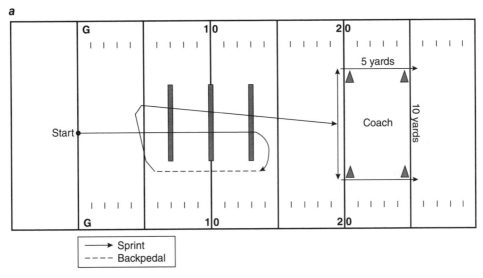

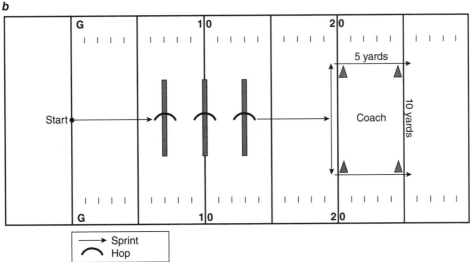

Figure 6.4 RACE Drills.

(continued)

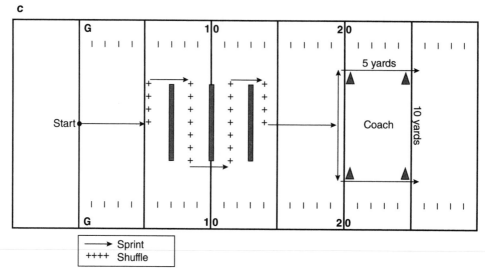

Figure 6.4 RACE Drills, *continued*.

- When you reach the cone before the coach, decelerate, keeping your eyes on the coach.
- The coach will point left or right to show you which way to go to finish the drill.

Five-Cone Drills

Equipment

- Five 12-inch cones
- Duct tape
- Measuring tape longer than 30 feet

Procedure

- Place four cones in a square, 10 yards away from each other. Use the tape measure if there are no lines to use. Place the fifth cone in the middle and measure the mark that is in the middle of two of the corner cones. Use the duct tape to mark the spot in case the cone is knocked over.
- Players progress through the 12 Five-Cone agility drills (figure 6.5), based on the progressions described in table 6.1.

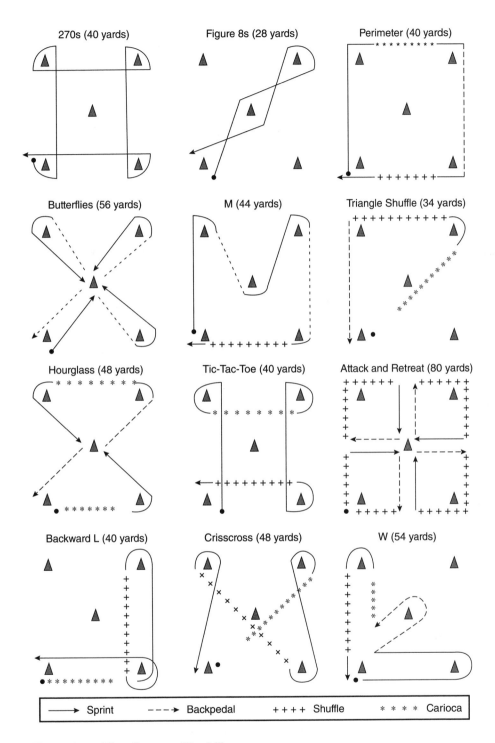

Figure 6.5   Five-Cone agility drills.

Table 6.1 Five-Cone Agility Drill Progressions

Week 1 (182 yards)	Week 2 (186 yards)	Week 3 (194 yards)	Week 4 (202 yards)
Figure 8s	Figure 8s	Figure 8s	Figure 8s
Triangle Shuffle	Triangle Shuffle	Triangle Shuffle	Triangle Shuffle
Perimeter	Perimeter	Perimeter	M
Tic-Tac-Toe	Tic-Tac-Toe	M	Crisscross
Backward L	M	Crisscross	Hourglass
Week 5 (206 yards)	**Week 6 (214 yards)**	**Week 7 (220 yards)**	**Week 8 (226 yards)**
Triangle Shuffle	Triangle Shuffle	Triangle Shuffle	Tic-Tac-Toe
Perimeter	Tic-Tac-Toe	Backward L	Perimeter
Backward L	M	M	M
M	Hourglass	Crisscross	Hourglass
Hourglass	Crisscross	W	W
Week 9 (230 yards)	**Week 10 (234 yards)**	**Week 11 (242 yards)**	**Week 12 (246 yards)**
Triangle Shuffle	Backward L	Tic-Tac-Toe	Tic-Tac-Toe
M	M	M	Hourglass
Hourglass	Hourglass	Hourglass	Crisscross
Crisscross	Crisscross	W	W
Butterflies	W	Butterflies	Butterflies
Week 13 (250 yards)	**Week 14 (254 yards)**	**Week 15 (260 yards)**	**Week 16 (264 yards)**
M	Triangle Shuffle	Tic-Tac-Toe	Triangle Shuffle
Hourglass	Backward L	Perimeter	Backward L
Crisscross	M	M	W
W	Butterflies	Butterflies	Butterflies
Butterfly	Attack and Retreat	Attack and Retreat	Attack and Retreat
Week 17 (270 yards)	**Week 18 (274 yards)**	**Week 19 (282 yards)**	**Week 20 (286 yards)**
Perimeter	Backward L	M	Hourglass
Tic-Tac-Toe	M	Hourglass	Crisscross
W	W	W	W
Butterflies	Butterflies	Butterflies	Butterflies
Attack and Retreat	Attack and Retreat	Attack and Retreat	Attack and Retreat

TESTING AGILITIES

The Pro Agility and Three-Cone drills (see chapter 2) are used to measure improvements in agility and are used as evaluations at the conclusion of the off-season and summer periods.

CONCLUSION

Like speed, agility can be improved year-round with proper planning. Closed drills provide a great basis for technical improvements in agility. Open drills such as the combo agilities give you gamelike movement patterns to prepare you for the season. Agility training must be viewed as high-intensity work as introduced in chapter 5.

Chapter 7

Power

For football players, training to be powerful is vital. They must be strong and able to move with speed. Strength training, which is described in chapter 8, is very important to develop and maximize power. Power, covered in this chapter, can be trained in the weight room as well as on the field. Performing exercises in the weight room with higher velocities develops power. Plyometric and medicine ball exercises are also great ways to develop power. In general, the more powerful you are, the better your chance for success on the field will be.

PLYOMETRICS

Before getting into plyometrics, we need to address athletic position. Proper athletic positioning allows you to maximize plyometric training as well as other forms of training, ensuring the effectiveness of each exercise and reducing the chance of injury. In the proper athletic position (figure 7.1), the center of gravity is over your feet with your ankles, knees, and hips flexed. Your feet are under your hips, and your back is arched. Your shoulders are back and your chest is out. Your head is positioned so your eyes can look straight ahead.

Plyometric training increases the rate of force development. Through a well-planned

Figure 7.1   Athletic position.

plyometric program, your muscles will allow more explosiveness. When performing plyometrics, you must allow sufficient recovery time. For training benefits to occur, each repetition must be done at 100 percent effort. Explosive properties in muscle fibers are diminished when you are fatigued. Therefore, full recovery between drills is mandatory. When performing these plyometric drills, follow your calendar in detail. A slow, gradual progression is necessary to prepare the muscles, tendons, and joints for higher-intensity exercises so you can gain the benefits without injury.

LOWER-BODY PLYOMETRICS

Balance Drills

Balance Drills are introductory plyometric exercises that teach athletic position as well as improve mobility and stability, reinforce proper landing mechanics, and train kinesthetic awareness. Single-leg balance drills may be performed with or without cues.

Procedure

- Start in the athletic position with one leg on the ground.
- Keep the opposite leg off the ground by flexing your hip and knee.
- Jump off the grounded foot and land on the opposite foot in the athletic position and pause. Do not let the lifted foot touch the ground.
- Jump back to the starting position and repeat.

Coaching Point

- Do these drills in all directions.

Broad Jump

The Broad Jump is a medium-intensity exercise. It can be performed with a repetitive option or a pause option.

Procedure

- Stand with slight flexion in your ankles, knees, and hips.
- Begin with your hands extended past your hips and your scapulae retracted (figure 7.2a). Drive your arms forward with force and drive off both feet to obtain maximum distance as you jump horizontally (figure 7.2b). Use a double arm action.
- Jump as far as possible. Flex your hips and knees to bring your feet under your buttocks.

- Land with both feet flat (figure 7.2c). Absorb force upon impact.
- If you choose to perform the exercise with the repetitive option, do not pause between jumps; minimize your ground contact time. If you choose the pause option, stop to regain your athletic position between jumps.

Figure 7.2   Broad Jump.

Diagonal Broad Jump

The Diagonal Broad Jump is a medium-intensity exercise. It can be performed with a repetitive option or a pause option.

Procedure

- Begin with your feet shoulder-width apart and your knees slightly flexed.
- Extend your hands past your hips and retract your scapulae. Drive your arms forward with force and drive off both feet to obtain maximum distance as you jump horizontally at a 45-degree angle. Take off at a 45-degree angle with an explosive two-foot jump. Use a double arm action.
- Jump as far as possible. Flex your hips and knees to bring your feet under your buttocks.
- Upon landing, perform the next jump at a 45-degree angle in the opposite direction. If you choose the repetitive option, do not pause between jumps and minimize your ground contact time. If you choose the pause option, stop to regain your athletic position between jumps.

Box Jump

The Box Jump is a low-intensity exercise.

Equipment

- Plyometric box

Procedure

- Stand with slight flexion in your ankles, knees, and hips behind a box. The box height is based on your ability to land on top of the box.
- Use a rapid countermovement. Extend your arms past your hips and then explosively drive them forward while extending at the hips and knees forcefully. Jump vertically using a double arm action.
- Jump as high as possible. Extend your hips and knees to bring your feet under your buttocks.
- Land with both feet flat on the box. Land softly and under control by flexing your ankles, knees, and hips to absorb the impact.

Lateral Box Jump

The Lateral Box Jump is a low-intensity exercise.

Equipment

- 12- to 24-inch plyometric box

Procedure

- Stand with slight flexion in your ankles, knees, and hips. Take your position with either your right or left side closer to the box. Stand as close to the box as you wish, although be sure to stand close enough so you can safely land with both feet on the box.
- Use a rapid countermovement. Jump up and land with both feet flat on the box. Jump vertically and use a double arm action.
- Jump as high as possible. Keep your shoulders square. Do not turn your hips.
- Land with both feet flat on the box. Land softly and under control by flexing your ankles, knees, and hips to absorb the impact.

Tuck Jump

The Tuck Jump is a medium-intensity exercise. It can be performed with a repetitive option or a maximum height option.

Procedure

- Stand with your feet shoulder-width apart in athletic position (figure 7.3*a*).
- Perform a rapid countermovement and jump as high as possible. Jump vertically and use a double arm action (figure 7.3*b*).
- Vigorously thrust your arms upward and flex your hips to bring your knees to your chest while pulling your heels to your buttocks.
- If you choose the repetitive option, do not pause between jumps and minimize your ground contact time. If you choose the max height option, gather yourself after landing and return to the ready position for the next repetition. This jump is repeated quickly. Your goal is to complete your repetitions as quickly as possible.

Figure 7.3   Tuck Jump.

Calf Shock Drop

The Calf Shock Drop is a medium-intensity exercise.

Equipment

- Stair step or 3- to 8-inch plyometric box

Procedure

- Stand fully upright on a stair step or 3- to 8-inch plyometric box facing away from the edge with your ankles dorsiflexed and your weight on the balls of your feet.
- Step back off the step or box with both feet and let gravity pull you to the landing surface.
- Maintain dorsiflexion as you land on the balls of your feet, absorbing the impact thorough your ankles.

Altitude Drop

The Altitude Drop is a medium- to high-intensity exercise, depending on box height.

Equipment

- Plyometric box

Procedure

- Stand on top of a plyometric box. The box should be no taller than your hips.
- Step—do not jump—off the box to let gravity pull you to the ground.
- Land on the balls of your feet, absorbing the impact through your ankle, knee, and hip. Minimize the jarring impact. Land as softly and smoothly as possible.
- After landing, extend your arms back with your scapulae retracted to the athletic position.

Depth Jump

The Depth Jump is a high-intensity exercise.

Equipment

- Plyometric box

Procedure

- Stand on top of a plyometric box. The box should be no taller than your hips.

- Step—do not jump—off the box and let gravity pull you to the ground.
- Land on the balls of your feet, absorbing the impact through your ankle, knee, and hip. Minimize the jarring impact. Land as softly and smoothly as possible.
- After landing, extend your arms back with your scapulae retracted to the athletic position. Use a rapid countermovement then explosively drive your arms forward while forcefully extending at the hips and knees. Spend less than 2 seconds on the ground. Jump either vertically or horizontally after landing.
- Use proper landing mechanics, and finish in the athletic position.

Squat Jump

The Squat Jump is a low- to medium-intensity exercise.

Procedure

- Place your palms on the back of your head. Stand with your feet shoulder-width apart, toes pointed slightly out. Get into an upright posture with your chest up, back flat, and head and eyes pointed slightly up.
- While keeping weight on your heels, begin squatting to the ground by pushing your hips back until you reach a parallel position (figure 7.4a).
- Once in the parallel position, quickly jump off the ground (figure 7.4b) by aggressively and simultaneously extending your hips, knees, and ankles.
- Land in the athletic position.

Figure 7.4   Squat Jump.

Split Jump

The Split Jump is a medium- to high-intensity exercise.

Procedure

- Stand with your feet in a split squat position with your knees slightly bent, feet evenly spaced apart, and toes pointing straight. Get into an upright posture with your chest up, back flat, and head and eyes pointed slightly up.
- Lower your body to the ground until your back knee is right above the ground.
- Once in this position, quickly jump off the ground by aggressively extending your hips, knees, and ankles simultaneously.
- While in the air, cycle your legs through and land in a quarter split squat position with your hips, knees, and ankles all slightly bent and the other leg forward.

Slide Board

The Slide Board is a medium- to high-intensity exercise.

Equipment

- Slide board
- Slide board booties

Procedure

- Stand in the athletic position on one end of the slide board.
- Use a rapid countermovement to push off the slide board block.
- Stay in the athletic position as you slide.
- When you reach the opposite block, change directions quickly and repeat.

UPPER-BODY PLYOMETRICS

Plyometric Push-Up

The Plyometric Push-Up is a medium-intensity exercise.

Equipment

- 6- to 20-pound medicine ball

Procedure

- Place both hands on the medicine ball and your feet on the ground.
- Bend your arms and touch your chest to the top of the medicine ball.
- Explode up with your arms, keeping your core tight, and pick the medicine ball up off the ground.
- When the medicine ball returns to the ground, repeat the exercise.

Coaching Point

- Hold on to the medicine ball at all times.

Medicine Ball Chest Pass

The Medicine Ball Chest Pass is a medium-intensity exercise.

Equipment

- 6- to 20-pound medicine ball.

Procedure

- Stand in the athletic position with the medicine ball in your hands at chest level.
- Explosively extend your arms as you throw the ball.
- Finish in the athletic position.

Coaching Point

- Keep your elbows close to your body and fully extend your arms.

Variations

- **Two-handed:** Stand in the athletic position, face a partner a body length away with feet shoulder-width apart and hands on both sides of the medicine ball, and throw from your chest.
- **Seated:** Sit in a straddle position facing your partner. Hold the medicine ball with your hands on both sides of the ball. Throw from your chest.
- **Staggered:** Stand with your feet staggered, your right foot in front of your left foot. Hold the medicine ball with your hands on both sides of the ball. Throw from your chest, keeping your feet stationary. Switch legs after half the reps are completed.
- **With step:** Stand with your feet staggered, your right foot in front of your left foot. Hold the medicine ball with your hands on both sides of the ball. Throw from your chest, stepping into the throw with your front leg. Switch legs after half the reps are completed.

- **Single leg:** Stand on one leg, facing your partner. Hold the medicine ball with your hands on both sides of the ball. Throw from your chest while maintaining your balance.
- **One arm:** Stand in the athletic position. Place one hand behind the ball, using the other hand on the side of the ball for balance. Pass the ball using only the hand behind the ball.

Overhead Throwdown

The Overhead Throwdown is a low-intensity exercise.

Procedure

- Stand in the athletic position facing your partner, feet shoulder-width apart.
- Hold the medicine ball with your hands on both sides, arms extended overhead.
- Throw the ball to the ground in front of your partner. Focus on using your trunk more than your arms to throw the ball.

Variations

- **Staggered:** Stand with your right leg in front of your left leg. Repeat with your left leg in front.
- **With step:** Stand with your right leg in front of your left leg. Step into the throw with your front leg. Repeat with your left leg in front.

OLYMPIC LIFTS

Olympic lifting can be an asset to any training program. Proper technique is most important to the success of Olympic lifts. Never sacrifice technique to lift a heavier weight. With proper technique, lifters of all ages may safely train using Olympic lifts.

Olympic lifting is great to train the triple extension of the ankles, knees, and hips. These lifts are also very good to develop power and explosiveness. While learning and training the Olympic lifts, make sure to learn how to escape a failed attempt by either walking out safely or pushing the bar away to avoid being trapped.

OLYMPIC LIFTS

Hang Clean

The Hang Clean is a multijoint exercise that builds explosive components in muscle. These components enhance the development of speed, power, jumping ability, muscle coordination, and quickness.

Starting Position

- Stand with your feet about shoulder-width apart.
- With your hands in a closed, pronated grip, grip the bar just outside your thighs.
- Set your core by raising your chest and drawing your navel in, hips back (figure 7.5*a*). Arch your back slightly.
- Curl your wrists so that your knuckles point to the floor, and turn your elbows out.

Starting Action

- Flex at your hip and knee until the bar is just above your kneecap (figure 7.5*b*).
- Maintain a slight arch in your back.
- Keep your shoulders over or slightly in front of the bar.
- Retract your scapulae (i.e., pull your shoulder blades back).
- Focus your eyes straight ahead or slightly up.
- Grip the bar with your arms hanging straight down.

Figure 7.5   Hang Clean.

(continued)

Figure 7.5 Hang Clean, *continued.*

Upward Movement

- Explosively drive your hips forward and up in a vertical jump movement (figure 7.5c).
- Extend at the ankles, knees, and hips (triple extension).
- Once you reach full triple extension, rapidly shrug your shoulders and then pull the bar with your arms, keeping your elbows high.

Downward Movement

- Once your lower body has fully extended and the bar has reached near-maximal height, pull your body under the bar and rotate your arms around and under the bar, shooting your elbows high. Simultaneously, flex your hips and knees into a squat position (figure 7.5d).
- Catch the bar, keeping your feet flat.

Variation

- Use the Tendo unit (see chapter 8) to add speed to the Hang Clean. Attach the Tendo unit to the bar before you get into the starting position. Use 1.4 m/s for heavy training, 1.55 m/s for medium training, and 1.7 m/s for light training.

Hang Shrug

The Hang Shrug is a variation of the Hang Clean that incorporates the triple extension with limited upper-body mechanics.

Starting Position

- Stand with your feet about shoulder-width apart.
- With your hands in a closed, pronated grip, grip the bar just outside your thighs.
- Set your core by raising your chest and drawing your navel in, hips back. Arch your back slightly (figure 7.6a).
- Curl your wrists so your knuckles point to the floor, and turn your elbows out.

First Movement

- Flex at your hip and knee until the bar is just above your kneecap (figure 7.6b).
- Maintain a slight arch in your back.
- Keep your shoulders over or slightly in front of the bar.
- Retract your scapulae (i.e., pull your shoulder blades back).
- Focus your eyes straight ahead or slightly up (figure 7.6c).

Upward Movement

- Explosively drive your hips forward and up in a vertical jump.
- Extend at the ankles, knees, and hips (triple extension).
- Once you reach full triple extension, rapidly shrug your shoulders up (figure 7.6d), but do not allow your elbows to flex at any time.

Figure 7.6   Hang Shrug.

(continued)

Figure 7.6 Hang Shrug, *continued.*

Downward Movement

- Simultaneously flex your hips and knees and allow the bar to return to the starting position.

High Pull

Basically, the High Pull is the Hang Clean without the catch.

Starting Position

- Stand with your feet about shoulder-width apart.
- With your hands in a closed, pronated grip, grip the bar just outside your thighs (figure 7.7*a*).
- Set your core by raising your chest and drawing your navel in, hips back. Arch your back slightly.
- Curl your wrists so your knuckles point to the floor, and turn your elbows out.

First Movement

- Flex at your hip and knee until the bar is just above your kneecap (figure 7.7*b*).
- Maintain a slight arch in your back.
- Keep your shoulders over or slightly in front of the bar.
- Retract your scapulae (i.e., pull your shoulder blades back).
- Focus your eyes straight ahead or slightly up (figure 7.7*c*).

Upward Movement

- Explosively drive your hips forward and up in a vertical jump.
- Extend at the ankles, knees, and hips (triple extension).
- Once you reach full triple extension, rapidly shrug your shoulders up and then pull with your arms, keeping your elbows high (figure 7.7*d*).
- Continue to drive your elbows as high as possible to achieve maximum bar height.

Downward Movement

- Simultaneously flex your hips and knees and allow the bar to return to the starting position.

Figure 7.7 High Pull.

Power Shrug

This exercise is very similar to the Hang Shrug except the pull is from the floor instead of right above the knee.

Starting Position

- Start with the bar on the ground.
- Walk toward the bar until your shins touch the bar.
- Stand with your feet about shoulder-width apart. Bend your ankles, knees, and hips, and lower yourself to grip the bar just outside your thighs with your hands in a closed, pronated grip.
- Set your core by raising your chest and drawing your navel in, hips back. Arch your back slightly.
- Curl your wrists so your knuckles point to the floor, and turn your elbows out.
- Keep your shoulders over or slightly in front of the bar.
- Retract your scapulae (i.e., pull your shoulder blades back).
- Focus your eyes straight ahead or slightly up.

Upward Movement

- Explosively drive your hips forward and up in a vertical jump.
- Extend at the ankles, knees, and hips (triple extension).
- Once you reach full triple extension, rapidly shrug your shoulders up, but do not allow your elbows to flex at any time.

Downward Movement

- Simultaneously flex your hips and knees, and allow the bar to return to the starting position.

MACHINE-BASED POWER EXERCISES

Jammer Extension

This exercise requires a Hammer Jammer machine. This is a multijoint exercise that builds explosive components in muscle. These components enhance speed, power, jumping ability, muscle coordination, and quickness.

Starting Position

- Position your feet about shoulder-width apart inside the machine.
- Using a closed, pronated grip, grab the handles.
- Fully extend your arms.
- Squat to a quarter-squat position (figure 7.8*a*).
- Set your back by sticking your chest out and your hips back. Arch your back slightly.
- Focus your eyes straight ahead.

Extension Movement

- Explosively drive your hips forward and up in a vertical jump movement (figure 7.8*b*).
- Flex your elbows to allow your chest to move forward.
- Forcefully extend at the ankles, knees, and hips (triple extension). Simultaneously drive your arms out and up, following the path of the machine.

Finish Position

- Finish with your ankles, knees, and hips fully extended. Your arms also should be fully extended. Imagine a straight, diagonal line from your hands down to your ankles.
- Your hips should rise before your shoulders.
- Maintain a flat back.
- Do not hold the finish position. You should be in the finish position for a split second before returning to the starting position.

Figure 7.8   Jammer Extension.

Downward Movement

- Gradually reduce the muscular tension in your arms to allow a controlled descent of the machine to its starting position.
- Simultaneously flex your hips, knees, and ankles.

Push/Pull Circuit

Ground-based machines are great for transferring power from the feet through the whole body into the hands. In this circuit, use six different ground-based machines (rotational, incline, and decline), one each for the left and right sides.

Starting Position

- Stand with your feet slightly wider than shoulder-width apart, using an even foot stance or a staggered stance.
- Begin in the athletic position with your ankles, knees, and hips flexed.
- Place both hands on the handles of the machine.

Starting Movement

- Simultaneously pull on the pull handle and push on the push handle.
- Be explosive by accelerating your moving arms as fast as possible.
- Make sure to have a tight grip on the handles.
- Quickly decelerate your moving arms as the push arm moves to full extension and the pull arm moves close to the body.

Finish Position

- Return to starting position after each repetition.
- Move to the next machine after the repetitions are complete.

CONCLUSION

It is important to establish a good base of strength to get the maximum benefit from power exercises. Training for power is accomplished by executing power exercises on the field or in the weight room with proper technique, effort, and speed. Training for power is training for explosiveness. The most dynamic football players are not only strong for their positions, but also very explosive. Using the right power exercises with good technique will allow you to dominate on the field.

Chapter 8

Strength

Training to be strong sets the foundation for football success in many ways. Football players need to be strong to reduce their risk of injury as well as to perform their tasks on the field. In general, football players who are the strongest at their positions will have the advantage on the field. Strength is not the most important trait to develop, although it is very important for success on the field.

POWER LIFTS

Traditionally, the Bench Press, Squat, and Dead Lift are considered power lifts. Powerlifting can be an asset to any training program as long as you keep in mind that proper technique is crucial. Never sacrifice technique to lift heavier weights because doing so could lead to injury. With proper technique, lifters of all ages may safely train using the power lifts. Powerlifting is great for training maximal motor recruitment as well as for building strength.

This glossary explains some powerlifting terms.

Tendo: This is a device used to measure bar speed by meters per second (m/s). It can be used to calculate maximum velocity, average velocity, and wattage. This device adds the dimension of velocity to lifts.

Naked: This is a term used to describe a lifting exercise without the addition of bands, chains, or any other external resistance to the bar.

Chains: Chains of various lengths, thicknesses, and weights can be added to the bar to create more external resistance. The chain adds load to the top of the lift and deloads during the descent. The lifter must accelerate the bar during the ascent as the load increases.

Bands: Large rubber bands of varying thicknesses and tensions can be attached to the bar and the lifting rack or bench. The band overloads the top of the movement similar to chains, but the band adds an overspeed component to the eccentric portion of the lift.

Maximum effort (ME): This term refers to training to lift maximal loads. (See *Science and Practice of Strength Training*, 2006, V. Zatsiorsky and William J. Kraemer, Human Kinetics: Champaign, IL.)

Dynamic effort (DE): This term refers to training with submaximal weights at maximal speed. This system improves rate of force development. The dynamic method is also known as speed work.

Repetitive effort (RE): This term refers to lifting a submaximal load to failure. During the final repetitions, the muscles produce the maximum force possible in a fatigued state. (For more information, see Louie Simmons of Westside Barbell at www.westside-barbell.com.)

Back Squat

The Back Squat develops hip, leg, and low back strength. This lift also strengthens the ligaments in the knees and assists in overall body development. Performing the Back Squat correctly will improve lower-body strength and enhance quickness, speed, and jumping ability.

Note: Wear a weight belt when executing Squats and Dead Lifts.

Starting Position

- Grasp the bar with a closed, pronated grip, hands slightly wider than shoulder width.
- Step under the bar and place the bar on your upper back and shoulders. Elevate your shoulders by contracting the trapezius.
- Squeeze your elbows down and under the bar to create a shelf for the bar, using the muscles of your upper back and shoulders.
- Pull your scapulae toward each other (i.e., pull your shoulder blades back).
- Tilt your head up slightly and focus your eyes on a target.
- Stand with your feet shoulder-width apart or wider; they should be even with each other, and your toes should point out slightly.
- Set your core by sticking your chest out and drawing your hips back (figure 8.1*a*). Your back should be flat or slightly arched.

Downward Movement

- Before the downward movement, inhale and hold your breath.
- Allow your hips and knees to slowly flex (figure 8.1*b*) while keeping your torso-to-floor angle relatively constant. Some torso flexion is appropriate.

- Maintain a flat or slightly arched back and keep your elbows high and your chest up and out.
- Keep your heels flat on the floor and your knees aligned over your feet.
- Do not round your back.
- Continue flexing your hips and knees until your thighs are parallel to the floor (figure 8.1c).
- Do not relax your torso at the bottom of the movement.

Figure 8.1   Back Squat.

Upward Movement

- During the upward movement, hold your breath until three-fourths of the way through the upward movement; then begin to exhale.
- Extend your hips and knees at the same rate. Do not allow your hips to rise before your chest.
- Maintain a flat back, keeping your elbows high and your chest up and out.
- Keep your heels flat on the floor and your knees aligned over your feet.
- Do not flex your torso forward or round your back.
- Continue extending your hips and knees (figure 8.1*d*) to reach the beginning position.
- Perform the ascent as explosively as possible.

Variation: Body Weight Squat

- Place your palms on the back of your head. Stand with your feet shoulder-width apart, toes pointed slightly out. Set your body in an upright posture with your chest up, back flat, and head and eyes pointed up slightly. While keeping weight on your heels, squat by pushing your hips back until your thighs are parallel to the ground. Once in the parallel position, actively extend your hips to return to the starting position while keeping weight on your heels.

Variation: Speed Squat

- Use the Tendo unit to add speed to the Back Squat. Attach the Tendo unit to the bar before you get into starting position. Recommended speeds are 0.6 m/s for heavy training, 0.8 m/s for medium training, and 1.0 m/s for light training.

Box Squat

Note: Wear a weight belt when executing Squats and Dead Lifts.

Starting Position

- Grasp the bar with a closed, pronated grip, hands slightly wider than shoulder width.
- Step under the bar and place the bar on your upper back and shoulders. Elevate your shoulders by contracting the trapezius.
- Squeeze your elbows down and under the bar to create a shelf for the bar, using the muscles of your upper back and shoulders.

- Pull your scapulae toward each other (i.e., pull your shoulder blades back).
- Tilt your head up slightly and focus your eyes on a target.
- Stand with your feet shoulder-width apart or wider; they should be even with each other and your toes should point out slightly.
- Set your core by sticking your chest out and drawing your hips back. Your back should be flat or slightly arched.
- Adjust the box height based on your body position. The box height can vary based on the depth desired.
- The box height can range so that the top or the bottom of your thighs are in a parallel position.

Downward Movement

- During the descent, move your hips back first.
- Keep your torso rigid while touching the box and ascend explosively.
- Do not sit and relax! Maintain a proper squat position with core rigidity.

Upward Movement

- During the upward movement, hold your breath until three-fourths of the way through the upward movement, then begin to exhale.
- Extend your hips and knees at the same rate. Do not allow your hips to rise before your chest.
- Maintain a flat back, keeping your elbows high and your chest up and out.
- Keep your heels flat on the floor and your knees aligned over your feet.
- Do not flex your torso forward or round your back.
- Continue extending your hips and knees to reach the starting position.
- Perform the ascent as explosively as possible.

Front Squat

The Front Squat develops hip, leg, and low back strength. This lift also strengthens the ligaments in your knees and helps in overall body development. Performing the Front Squat correctly improves lower-body strength and enhances quickness, speed, and jumping ability.

Note: Wear a weight belt when executing Squats and Dead Lifts.

Starting Position

- Using a closed, pronated grip, grasp the bar with hands slightly wider than shoulder width.
- Step to the bar and place the bar on top of the anterior deltoids (front of the shoulders) and clavicles (collarbones)(figure 8.2*a*).
- Fully flex your elbows to position your upper arms parallel to the floor (figure 8.2*b*).
- Lift your elbows to create a shelf for the bar using the anterior deltoids.
- Hold your chest up and out.
- Pull your scapulae toward each other.
- Tilt your head up slightly.
- Position your feet shoulder-width apart or wider; they should be even with each other, and your toes should point out slightly.
- Set your back by sticking your chest and butt out. Your back should be flat or slightly arched.

Downward Movement

- Inhale and hold your breath before the downward movement.
- Allow your hips and knees to flex slowly while keeping your torso-to-floor angle relatively constant. Some torso flexion is appropriate.
- Maintain a flat or slightly arched back, keeping your elbows high and your chest up and out.
- Keep your heels flat on the floor and your knees aligned over your feet.
- Do not round your back.
- Continue flexing your hips and knees until your thighs are parallel to the floor (figure 8.2*c*).
- Do not relax your torso at the bottom of the movement.

Upward Movement

- Hold your breath until three-fourths of the way through the upward movement; then begin to exhale.

- Extend your hips and knees at the same rate. Do not allow your hips to rise before your chest.
- Maintain a flat back, keeping your elbows high and your chest up and out.
- Keep your heels flat on the floor and your knees aligned over your feet (figure 8.2*d*).
- Do not flex your torso forward or round your back.
- Continue extending your hips and knees to reach the beginning position.

Figure 8.2   Front Squat.

Extended Squat

The Extended Squat is also a great mobility exercise when using very light weights. This exercise is very similar to regular Back Squats except the bar is in a pressed overhead position.

Note: Wear a weight belt when executing Squats and Dead Lifts.

Starting Position

- Grasp the bar with a closed, pronated grip. Your elbows and shoulders should be at 90-degree angles.
- Pick up the bar with your arms fully extended overhead.
- Tilt your head up slightly and focus your eyes on a target.
- Stand with feet shoulder-width apart; they should even with each other, and your toes should point out slightly.
- Set your core by sticking your chest out and drawing your hips back. Your back should be flat or slightly arched.

Downward Movement

- Before the downward movement, inhale and hold your breath.
- Allow your hips and knees to slowly flex while keeping your torso-to-floor angle relatively constant. Some torso flexion is appropriate.
- Keep your heels flat on the floor and your knees aligned over your feet.
- Do not round your back.
- Continue flexing your hips and knees until your thighs are parallel to the floor (figure 8.3).
- Do not relax your torso at the bottom of the movement.

Upward Movement

- During the upward movement, hold your breath until three-fourths of the way through the upward movement; then begin to exhale.
- Extend your hips and knees at the same rate. Do not allow your hips to rise before your chest.
- Keep your heels flat on the floor and your knees aligned over your feet.
- Do not flex your torso forward or round your back. Keep the bar overhead.
- Continue extending your hips and knees to reach the beginning position.
- Perform the ascent under control.

Figure 8.3   Extended Squat.

Dead Lift

The Dead Lift is a total-body exercise that emphasizes the glutes, quads, and back extensors.

Note: Wear a weight belt when executing Squats and Dead Lifts.

Starting Position

- Stand with your feet flat and hip-width apart, toes pointing out slightly.
- Squat down and grasp the bar with an alternated grip (one hand turned out, the other turned in) (figure 8.4*a*).
- Keep your back flat or slightly arched, the trapezius relaxed and slightly stretched.
- Hold your chest up and out, scapulae retracted, with your head in line with your vertebral column or hyperextended slightly, heels in contact with the floor.
- Keep your shoulders over or slightly in front of the bar, eyes focused straight ahead or slightly up.

Upward Movement

- Lift the bar off the floor by extending your hips and knees (figure 8.4*b*).
- Keep your torso-to-floor angle constant.
- Do not let your hips rise before your shoulders.
- Maintain a flat back.

- Keep your elbows fully extended, your head neutral in relation to the vertebral column, and your shoulders over the bar.
- Once the bar passes knee level, extend at the back while continuing with knee and hip extension.
- At full knee and hip extension, establish an erect body position (figure 8.4c).
- Perform the ascent as explosively as possible.

Downward Movement

- Allow your hips and knees to flex to slowly lower the bar to the floor (figure 8.4d).
- Maintain a flat back. Do not flex your torso forward.

Figure 8.4   Dead Lift.

Bench Press

The Bench Press strengthens the pectoralis major muscles of the chest and the triceps. This exercise also can be performed with two dumbbells and a closed, pronated grip.

Starting Position

- Lie on the weight bench in a five-point body contact position: your head, shoulders, and hips are in contact with the weight bench. Your feet should be flat on the floor.
- Position yourself on the bench so that your eyes are below the edge of the supports.
- Grasp the bar with a closed, pronated grip.
- Place the bar over your chin with your elbows fully extended (figure 8.5a).

Downward Movement

- Inhale during the downward movement.
- Lower the bar to touch your chest at approximately midchest level (figure 8.5b).
- Keep your elbows close to your body by contracting the latissimus as you would when performing a Lat Pulldown.
- Keep your wrists rigid and directly above your elbows.
- Maintain the five-point body contact position.

Upward Movement

- Exhale through the sticking point of the upward movement.
- Push the bar up and slightly back. The bar should travel in a slight arc.

 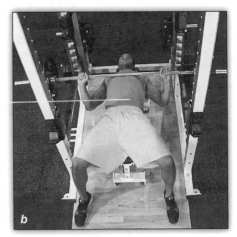

Figure 8.5   Bench Press.

- Keep your wrists rigid and directly above your elbows.
- Maintain the five-point body contact position. Do not arch your back or lift your butt off the bench.
- Perform the ascent as explosively as possible.

Variation: Speed Press

- Use the Tendo unit to add speed to the Bench Press. Attach the Tendo unit to the bar before you get into starting position. Recommended speeds are 0.6 m/s for heavy training, 0.8 m/s for medium training, and 1.0 m/s for light training.

Board Bench Press

For the Board Bench Press, stack one to five 2-by-6-inch boards to limit the bench stroke. Limiting the range of motion allows you to use more weight than you could with a full range of motion. You will need a partner to hold the board on your chest.

Equipment

- Glue and screw each 2-by-6 board together. The board's total height will range from 2 to 10 inches. Make sure the boards are at least 2 feet long and have a handle.

Starting Position

- Lie on the weight bench in a five-point body contact position with your head, shoulders, and hips in contact with the weight bench. Your feet should be flat on the floor.
- Position yourself on the bench so that your eyes are below the edge of the supports.
- Grasp the bar with a closed, pronated grip.
- Place the bar over your chin with your elbows fully extended.

Downward Movement

- Inhale before the downward movement.
- Lower the bar to touch the boards at approximately midchest level.
- Keep your elbows close to your body by contracting the latissimus as you would when performing a Lat Pulldown.
- Keep your wrists rigid and directly above your elbows.
- Maintain the five-point body contact position.

Upward Movement

- Exhale through the sticking point of the upward movement.
- Push the bar up and slightly back. The bar should travel in a slight arc.
- Keep your wrists rigid and directly above your elbows.
- Maintain the five-point body contact position. Do not arch your back or lift your butt off the bench.
- Perform the ascent as explosively as possible.

Floor Press

Starting Position

- Set up the bar in a rack so you will have a safe liftoff.
- Lie supine on the floor in a seven-point body contact position with your head, shoulders, hips, and feet in contact with the floor. Your feet should be flat on the floor.
- Position yourself on the floor so that your eyes are below the edge of the supports.
- Grasp the bar with a closed, pronated grip.
- Place the bar over your chin with your elbows fully extended.

Downward Movement

- Inhale before the downward movement.
- Lower the bar to touch your elbows on the floor.
- Keep your elbows close to your body by contracting the latissimus as you would when performing a Lat Pulldown.
- Keep your wrists rigid and directly above your elbows.
- Maintain the seven-point body contact position.

Upward Movement

- Exhale through the sticking point of the upward movement.
- Push the bar up and slightly back. The bar should travel in a slight arc.
- Keep your wrists rigid and directly above your elbows.
- Maintain the seven-point body contact position. Do not arch your back or lift your butt off the floor.
- Perform the ascent as explosively as possible.

Strongman

Strongman exercises develop strength and overall conditioning. When choosing an implement, consider these questions:

- How far?
- How much time?
- How much weight?
- Is it a competition?
- How many repetitions and sets?

All of the equipment mentioned in the following exercises can be made or purchased online or through a catalog.

Exercises

Farmer's Walk: Hold an implement in each hand and walk or run a specified distance.

Yoke Carry: Carry a yoke on your back for a specified distance.

Stone Lift: Lift a large stone or heavy medicine ball off the ground and place it onto a higher surface.

Tire Flip: Perform this exercise alone or recruit one or two partners, depending on the size of the tires. Using large tractor tires, lift up one side of the tire and flip it over until it lands flat on the opposite side.

Prowler: Using a weighted sled with handles, perform pushes and pulls.

Plate Push: Use a steel plate and a flat surface. Place your hands on a plate that is lying flat on the ground and push it a certain distance.

Sled Pull: Attach a harness or belt to a weighted sled. Walk forward, backward, or laterally for a specified distance.

BODYBUILDING

Use bodybuilding to isolate certain muscles and muscle groups or joints to improve strength, size, or function. Bodybuilding consists of high volume using low to moderate weights. Isometric, concentric, and eccentric contractions, and manual resistance are used. Many of these exercises will help you push past your limits. Often a partner is allowed to assist you. These exercises will add variety and excitement to your workouts.

This glossary explains methods that can be used to build muscle hypertrophy, also known as bodybuilding.

Strip sets: These exercises start with no weight on the bar or the maximum amount of weight you can handle on the bar. First, establish the exercise and number of repetitions; then, whether to move up or down in weight. For instance, if doing the Bench Press (page 131), start with four or five 5-, 10-, or 25-pound plates on each side of the bar, perform 5 to 8 reps, remove a plate from each side, complete another 5 to 8 reps, and so on, until the bar is unloaded. Once the bar is unloaded, terminate the set or start the accent by adding a plate every 5 to 8 reps until you can't perform anymore reps by yourself. At this point, the spotter can help you complete the set. Strip sets can be performed with Shrugs, Biceps Curls, Triceps Extensions, Back Rows, Squats, and so on.

Work the rack: Perform these exercises at the dumbbell (DB) rack. First, establish the exercise, number of reps, and direction. For instance, if the exercise is the Arnold Shoulder Press (page 163), select the starting weight and determine the weight increase. Start with a 5-pound dumbbell, do 5 reps, and replace the dumbbell on the rack. Next, pick up the 10-pound dumbbell and do 5 reps, continuing this way up to the determined limit. Then return to the 5-pound dumbbell by reducing the weight each set by 5-pound increments. This can also be done from heavy to light to heavy. Work the rack with One-Arm Rows, Biceps Curls, Triceps Extensions, Squats, Dead Lifts, Single-Arm Bench Presses, and so on.

Work the stack: These exercises are performed using a selectorized cable pulley machine. First, establish the exercise, number of reps, and direction. For instance, if the exercise is the Lat Pulldown (page 155), select the starting weight and determine the weight increase. It helps to have a partner move the pin up and down when you work the stack to keep you on pace and provide encouragement. Start with a moderate weight and work up the stack to the lightest weight before returning down the stack until you cannot physically complete another rep. Work the stack exercises include any exercise that can be performed on any selectorized piece of equipment.

Iso holds: Isometric exercises are exercises in which no movement occurs; however, resistance is needed for maintaining position.

Towel exercises: Many exercises can be performed with a towel. The towel allows for partner manual resistance through eccentric and concentric movement. Isometric exercises also can be performed using a towel. Towel work also trains the grip with good efficiency. Partner towel exercises include Biceps Curls, Triceps Extensions, and Back Rows. Towel Hangs for time are great for training the grip.

CORE

The core can be trained in a variety of ways. Use as much variety as possible, and always pay attention to your core positioning during the exercise.

Ab Circuits

Circuits are great for targeting different areas of the core. Assemble two or more abdominal exercises and do 15 to 20 reps each to create a circuit like in figure 8.6.

Exercises

Crunch: Lie supine on the ground with your knees bent. Reach through your legs with your arms. Lift your upper back off the ground and return to the starting position.

Reverse Crunch: Lie supine on the ground. Lift and bend your knees, bringing them toward your chest. Return your legs to the ground.

Rotation: Lie supine on the ground with your knees bent. Lift your low back off the ground and rotate your upper torso. Touch both hands on the ground next to your hips. Go back and forth.

Oblique Crunch: Lie supine on the ground with your knees bent. Lift your torso off the ground and touch your right shoe with your right hand then touch your left shoe with your left hand. Go back and forth.

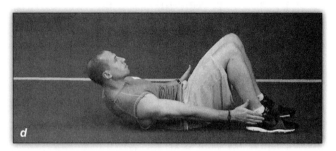

Hanging Knee Raise: Grab the grips of a pull-up bar and let your body hang. Lift your knees to your chest and slowly lower your legs back to the starting position.

Figure 8.6   Ab Circuit.

MOBILITY

Mobility is the range of motion revolving primarily around the ankle, hip, and thoracic joint areas. This requires proper motor and muscular function. With improved mobility, you will be able to perform skills at higher and more efficient levels.

Hurdles

Stepover

- Place 5 to 10 hurdles in a row.
- Facing the hurdles, lift your lead leg over and then lift your trail leg over.
- Repeat with the lead leg until you go through all of the hurdles.
- Do not allow your foot to swing to the outside of the hurdle.

Step-Through

- Place 5 to 10 hurdles in a row.
- Stand with your right or left foot next to the first hurdle.
- Flex your ankle, knees, and hips and step laterally under the first hurdle.
- Bring your trail leg under and stand up in between hurdles.
- Repeat using the same lead foot until you go through all the hurdles.

Band X-Walk

Procedure

- Place a medium-strength band around the arches of both feet and in both hands to make a large X.
- Step laterally with your lead leg (figure 8.7) and follow with your trail leg laterally.
- Adjust the tension by using your hands and arms to raise or lower the band.

Figure 8.7   Band X-Walk.

Leg Swing

Hip Extension and Flexion

- Stand on one leg. Support your body with the opposite hand against a wall for balance.
- Freely swing your leg forward and backward, trying to get greater range of motion with each swing.
- Keep your torso upright and your leg straight and relaxed for the best results. Do not bend at the waist.
- Perform 10 reps.

Abduction and Adduction

- Stand on one leg. Support your body with both hands against a wall.
- Freely swing your leg laterally across your body and out, trying to get greater range of motion with each swing.
- Keep your torso upright and your leg straight and relaxed for best results. Do not bend at the waist.
- Perform 10 reps.

STABILITY

Stability is required at certain joint areas in the body. Three of the most important areas that require stability are your knees, core, and shoulders. The muscle groups surrounding these areas have to function synergistically to produce and absorb forces properly.

ROTATOR CUFF

Cable External Rotation

To perform the Cable External Rotation, place a rolled towel in your armpit and squeeze it to your rib cage.

Procedure

- Stand approximately 2 feet away from the weight stack with your hip perpendicular to the stack, feet shoulder-width apart.
- Begin with your elbow pinned at your side and flexed to 90 degrees. Hold the cable handle across your abdomen with your shoulder internally rotated (figure 8.8a).

- Keeping your elbow flexed and at your side, externally rotate your shoulder, pulling the cable handle to the side of your body and parallel to the floor (figure 8.8*b*).

Figure 8.8   Cable External Rotation.

Cable Internal Rotation

Procedure

- Stand approximately 2 feet away from the weight stack with your hip perpendicular to the stack, feet shoulder-width apart.
- Begin with your elbow pinned at your side and flexed to 90 degrees. Hold the cable handle with your shoulder externally rotated and the handle out to the side of your body (figure 8.9*a*).

Figure 8.9   Cable Internal Rotation.

- Keeping your elbow flexed and at your side, internally rotate your shoulder, pulling the cable handle across your abdomen (figure 8.9b).

Full Can

Procedure

- Stand with your feet shoulder-width apart, knees slightly bent. Hold dumbbells outside of your thighs with your wrist supinated and your thumbs up.
- With your arm extended, flex your shoulder to lift the dumbbells at a 45-degree angle from your body.
- Lower the dumbbells to the starting position.

Cuban Press

Procedure

- Holding the dumbbells, lift your arms until your elbows and shoulders are at 90 degrees (figure 8.10a).
- Externally rotate your shoulders until your hands are upright (figure 8.10b).
- Press your hands up until your arms are fully extended (figure 8.10c).
- Reverse the progression until you are back to the starting position.

Figure 8.10 Cuban Press.

Scap Circuit

The Scap Circuit is a supplemental exercise that isolates the scapulae to promote proper function of the shoulders. This circuit is a key component to increasing the integrity of the rotator cuff. The circuit is made up of four exercises performed in a row. Perform 10 repetitions of each exercise.

Equipment

- Exercise band or cable machine
- Barbell
- Pull-up bar

Scap Push-Up

- Begin in the starting position of a push-up with your elbows fully extended.
- While maintaining full extension of your elbows, retract your scapula (i.e., bring your shoulder blades together).
- Actively protract your scapulae (i.e., push your shoulder blades apart) while maintaining full extension of your elbows to return to the starting position.

Scap Band Row

- Begin in an upright, seated position.
- Grab the band or cable machine attachment with a supinated grip with your elbows in full extension.
- While maintaining full extension of your elbows, actively pull your shoulders down and back by depressing and retracting your scapulae (i.e., bring your shoulder blades together).
- Hold for a three count and slowly return to the starting position.

Overhead Shrug

- Begin in a standing position.
- Grasp the bar with a closed, pronated grip. Your elbows and shoulders should be at 90-degree angles.
- Actively shrug the barbell up by elevating your scapulae while maintaining a perfect standing posture and full extension of your elbows.
- Hold for a three count and slowly return to the starting position.

Scap Chin-Up

- Grab a pull-up bar with a shoulder-width, neutral grip and shoulders in full extension.
- While maintaining a slight bend at your elbows, actively depress and retract your scapulae (i.e., bring your shoulder blades together).
- Hold for a three count and slowly return to the starting position by protracting your scapulae (i.e., push your shoulder blades apart).

Bridge Series

Front Bridge

- Begin in a prone position on the floor with your weight resting on your forearms with your elbows tight to your sides.
- Your body should be in a perfectly straight line with your ankles dorsiflexed into the ground (figure 8.11a).
- The goal is to remain as stable as possible.

Back Bridge

- Begin in a supine position.
- Raise and elevate your body by pushing your hands down into the ground with your arms fully extended.
- Actively squeeze your glutes to push your hips to their highest point (figure 8.11b).
- Your heels should be pressed into the ground while your ankles remain dorsiflexed.
- The goal is to remain as stable as possible.

Side Bridge (Right and Left)

- Begin in a lateral position on either your right (figure 8.11c) or left side (figure 8.11d).
- Your body must remain in a perfectly straight line with your weight resting on your forearm.
- Stack your feet on top of each other while keeping your hips in a neutral position with your spine.
- The goal is to remain as stable as possible.

Figure 8.11   Bridge Series.

LOWER BODY

Many exercises can be used to train the lower body. It is important to know which lower-body exercises will enhance your program. Following are some exercises that assist with lower-body strength development.

DOUBLE LEG

Leg Extension

The Leg Extension isolates and strengthens the quadriceps muscles.

Starting Position

- Sit down in a leg extension machine and press your back firmly against the back pad.
- Place your ankles behind and in contact with the foot roller pad.
- Position your legs parallel to each other.
- Align your knees with the axis of the machine.
- Grasp the handles on the machine (figure 8.12*a*).

Upward Movement

- Exhale on the upward movement.
- Raise the roller pad by fully extending your knees (figure 8.12*b*).
- Keep your torso erect and your back firmly pressed against the back pad.
- Maintain a tight grip on the handles.
- Do not allow your hips or buttocks to lift off the seat.

Downward Movement

- Inhale on the downward movement.
- Allow your knees to flex slowly back to the beginning position.
- Keep your torso erect and your back firmly pressed against the back pad.
- Maintain a tight grip on the handles.

Figure 8.12   Leg Extension.

SINGLE LEG

Walking Lunge

The Walking Lunge develops the gluteus maximus and the hamstrings. You also can use dumbbells when performing this exercise. Allow the dumbbells to hang at your sides.

Starting Position

- Using a closed, pronated grip, grasp the bar with your hands slightly wider than shoulder width.
- Place the bar in a balanced position on your upper back and shoulders at the base of your neck.
- Hold your chest up and out.
- Pull your scapulae toward each other (i.e., pull your shoulder blades back).
- Tilt your head up slightly.
- Position your feet parallel to each other.

Forward Movement

- Using your lead leg, take one exaggerated step directly forward (figure 8.13a).
- Keep your torso erect as your lead foot moves.

Figure 8.13   Walking Lunge.

- Keep your lead knee and foot aligned, toes pointing straight ahead.
- Plant your lead foot squarely on the floor.
- Flex your lead knee and hip slowly and under control. Do not allow the knee of your trailing leg to touch the ground.
- Lower the knee of your trailing leg toward the floor.
- Keep your torso vertical to the floor by sitting back on your trailing leg.
- Keep your lead knee directly over your lead foot, shin perpendicular to the floor.
- Keep your lead foot flat on the floor.
- Do not bounce at the bottom position.
- Inhale during the forward movement phase.

Walking Movement

- Forcefully drive your trailing leg off the floor by extending your lead hip and knee.
- Continue walking in this position (figure 8.13*b*). Try not to break stride.
- Maintain an erect torso.
- Exhale during the push-off of the walking movement phase.

Step-Up

The Step-Up develops hip and leg strength. You also can use dumbbells when performing this exercise. Allow the dumbbells to hang at your sides.

Note: Use a 12- to 18-inch box or a box high enough to create a 90-degree angle at your knee joint when your foot is on the box.

Starting Position

- Using a closed, pronated grip, grasp the bar with your hands slightly wider than shoulder width.
- Step under the bar and place the bar on your upper back and shoulders (figure 8.14*a*).
- Lift your elbows to create a shelf for the bar using your upper back and shoulder muscles.
- Hold your chest up and out.
- Pull your scapulae toward each other.
- Tilt your head up slightly.

Upward Movement

- Exhale through the sticking point of the upward movement.
- Step up with your lead leg and place your entire foot on top of the box. The toes of your lead leg point straight ahead (figure 8.14b).
- Do not lean forward.
- Shift your body weight to your lead leg.
- Push with your lead leg to move your body to a standing position on top of the box (figure 8.14c).
- Do not push off with your trailing leg.
- Maintain an erect body position.
- At the top position, your hips and knees should be fully extended.

Downward Movement

- Inhale before the downward movement.
- Keep your body weight on the same lead leg.
- With the same trailing leg, step off the box.
- Maintain an erect body position.
- At full trail foot contact, shift your body weight to your trailing leg.
- Pick up your lead leg and place it back on the box to repeat the upward movement phase.

Figure 8.14   Step-Up.

Pistol Squat

Procedure

- Use a bench or box and hold a weighted object in your hands for counterbalance.
- Lift one leg off the floor. Move your hips back and slowly lower your body until your glutes are touching the box or bench (figure 8.15).
- Make sure your back is arched and your chest is up the entire time.
- Lower to the box in a controlled motion. Sit softly and maintain your position. Do not relax.
- Maintain your balance as you return to the starting position.

Figure 8.15   Pistol Squat.

Split Squat

Procedure

- Assume a lunge position with your feet. Slowly lower your back knee to the floor by flexing it (figure 8.16).
- Do not allow your back knee to crash to the floor.
- Make sure your front knee does not extend past your front toes.
- Push up until both legs are at the starting position.
- Perform equal reps by switching the lead foot.

Figure 8.16   Split Squat.

Plate Push

Equipment

- Flat-sided weight plate (45, 25, or 10 pounds)

Procedure

- Evenly place both hands on a weight plate that is flat on the floor. Your elbows should be fully extended. Hold your head in a neutral position with your weight on the balls of your feet.
- Initiate the movement by forcefully and actively driving your knee upward toward your elbow by flexing your hip while simultaneously extending the opposite leg.
- Repeat until you achieve the prescribed distance or time.

Overhead Stair Walk

Equipment

- Weight plate
- Stairs

Procedure

- Press a plate directly overhead and then hold it in this position with your arms fully extended.
- Walk up steps while maintaining an upright posture with the plate held overhead.
- Keep the plate overhead with your arms fully extended until you achieve the prescribed distance or time.

POSTERIOR CHAIN

The posterior chain refers to the low back, glutes, and hamstrings.

Romanian Dead Lift (RDL)

The Romanian Dead Lift strengthens the spinal erectors in the low back, the glutes, and the hamstrings. This exercise will help reduce hamstring strains as well as aid in speed development. You may use dumbbells instead of a barbell to perform this exercise.

Starting Position

- Grab the bar using an alternate grip (one hand turned out, the other turned in).
- Position your feet slightly wider than shoulder-with apart (figure 8.17a).
- Slightly bend your knees.
- Set your back by sticking your chest out and your hips back. Your back should be slightly arched.
- Squeeze your shoulder blades together.

Downward Movement

- Maintaining your posture, slowly move your hips back past your heels and allow your torso to slowly flex forward and the bar to lower toward the floor (figure 8.17b).
- Maintain an arched back and keep your weight on your heels.
- Lower the bar to shin level.
- You should feel the hamstrings stretch.

Upward Movement

- Extend your hips and torso by driving your hips forward, raising the weight until you are standing upright, back in the starting position (figure 8.17c).
- Keep your knees slightly flexed and your torso in a flat-back position.
- Do not jerk your torso.

Figure 8.17 Romanian Dead Lift.

Hyperextension

Procedure

- Get into a prone position with your feet locked into a hyperextension machine and your arms across your chest.
- Lower your body to 90 degrees and slowly raise your body until parallel to the floor. Squeeze your glutes hard at extension.
- Do not rise past parallel. Your hips should be level with the pads of the hyperextension machine.

Reverse Hyperextension

This exercise can be done with a specially designed piece of equipment that allows you to add resistance. You can also do it with a medicine ball between your feet to add resistance.

Procedure

- Get into a prone position, lying across the pads (figure 8.18*a*).
- Hold the handles to secure your upper body.
- Your lower body is free with your hips just off the pads.
- Keeping your legs straight, raise your legs to a parallel position (figure 8.18*b*) and lower to the starting position.
- Your hips should not bounce off the pad.

Figure 8.18   Reverse Hyperextension.

Leg Curl

The Leg Curl isolates and strengthens the hamstrings as knee flexors. A leg (knee) curl machine is needed for performing this exercise.

Procedure

- Place the pad of the leg curl machine just above your ankles.
- Place your back against the machine's back support, if needed. Make sure your body is in a position to maximize range of motion.
- Flex your knee with as much range of motion as possible.
- Allow your movement leg to return slowly to the starting position.

Good Morning

Starting Position

- Stand with your feet slightly wider than shoulder-width apart.
- Lift the bar to the Back Squat position. Place the bar on your upper back and shoulders, hold your chest up and out, and pull your scapulae toward each other.

Starting Movement

- Move your hips back.
- Bend at the waist (figure 8.19a).

Downward and Upward Movements

- As the bar lowers, move your hips farther back until your torso is almost parallel to the ground.
- Contract your hamstrings and glutes to raise the bar until you return to the fully upright position (figure 8.19b).

Figure 8.19 Good Morning.

Glute Ham Raise

Beginning Position and Movement

- Place your feet in the foot pads of a glute ham bench.
- Start with your knees bent in a 90-degree position with your torso upright (figure 8.20*a*).
- Unlock your knees and straighten your legs without bending at the waist.

Downward and Upward Movements

- Straighten your knees, keeping your torso rigid, stopping once your body is fully straight and parallel to the ground (figure 8.20*b*).
- Initiate the upward movement by contracting your hamstrings, glutes, and low back muscles.
- Do not bend at the waist. Bend only at your knees until your torso is fully upright.

Figure 8.20 Glute Ham Raise.

UPPER BODY

Upper-body exercises support and stabilize the shoulders. Upper-back training will help absorb the pressing and collision forces that football players are exposed to. In a workout always try to balance the number of pressing and pulling exercises. A good rule of thumb is twice as many pulling repetitions as pushing repetitions. Upper-back exercises are considered pulling exercises.

BACK

High Lat Pulldown

The High Lat Pulldown strengthens the latissimus dorsi, middle trapezius, and rhomboids of the upper back.

Starting Position

- Grasp the bar of a high lat pulldown machine. Grips can vary based on personal preference.
- Sit down on the machine so that your body is anchored.
- Position your thighs under the pads with your feet flat on the floor. If necessary, adjust the seat and thigh pad.
- Fully extend your arms.

Downward Movement

- Exhale on the downward movement.
- Pull the bar or machine arms down and toward your upper chest. Do not jerk your torso to assist the movement.
- Touch the bar to your upper chest.

Upward Movement

- Inhale on the upward movement.
- Allow your elbows to slowly extend back to the starting position.
- Keep your torso in the same position.

One-Arm Dumbbell Row

The One-Arm Dumbbell Row strengthens the latissimus dorsi, teres major, middle trapezius, and rhomboids of the back.

Starting Position

- Kneel on the weight bench with your inside leg.
- Lean forward and support your upper torso with your inside hand on the bench.
- Place your outside foot at the side of the bench and flex your knee.
- Position your torso parallel to the floor.
- Grasp the dumbbell with your outside hand.
- Hold the dumbbell at full elbow extension.

Upward Movement

- Exhale on the upward movement.
- Pull the dumbbell up toward your hip and ribs.
- Keep your upper arm and elbow close to your torso.
- Keep your back and shoulders even and parallel to the floor.
- Keep your torso rigid and your back flat.

Downward Movement

- Inhale on the downward movement.
- Allow your elbow to slowly extend back to the starting position.
- Keep your torso in the same position.

Low Row

The Low Row strengthens the latissimus dorsi, teres major, middle trapezius, and rhomboids of the back.

Starting Position

- Assume a seated position on a low row machine.
- Place your feet on the machine frame or foot supports.
- Grasp the bar or grips on the machine. Grips can vary based on personal preference.
- Sit erect with a rigid torso and your back perpendicular to the floor.
- Allow your elbows to extend fully (figure 8.21a).

Backward (Concentric) Movement

- Exhale during the backward movement.
- Pull the handles toward your chest or abdomen (figure 8.21*b*).
- Maintain an erect torso position and keep your elbows next to your ribs.
- Pull the handles as far back as possible.
- Do not jerk your torso to assist the move.

Forward (Eccentric) Movement

- Inhale during the forward movement.
- Keeping your elbows next to your ribs, allow the handles to move back to the starting position.
- Keep your torso in the same position.

Figure 8.21   Low Row.

Pull-Up

Procedure

- Using an overhand grip, hang from a pull-up bar with your hands shoulder-width apart and your arms fully extended.
- Pull your body up until your chin clears the bar. Return to the starting position.
- Focus on keeping your body steady (no swinging or kicking).

Variations

- Use a closed-supinated grip (chin-up), a neutral grip (parallel grip), an alternating grip (one-hand reverse grip, one-hand closed grip), a narrow grip (6 inches between hands, closer than shoulder width), or a wide grip (wider than shoulder width).
- Hold your legs at a 90-degree angle in front to perform a 90-Degree Straight-Leg Pull-Up.
- For a partner-assisted pull-up, have your partner spot you at the rib cage.
- For a machine-assisted pull-up, set the machine at the desired assisted weight.

Barbell Row

Starting Position and Movement

- Stand with your feet slightly wider than shoulder-width apart.
- Move your hips back and bend at the waist.
- Let the bar hang with your arms straight.
- Perform a Bent-Over Row with the barbell (figure 8.22)
- Your hands are one hand width wider than shoulders width.
- Use an underhand or overhand grip.

Figure 8.22   Barbell Row.

Upward Movement

- Pull the bar up until the barbell touches your chest.
- Squeeze your scapulae together.

Downward Movement

- Slowly and under control lower the bar to the starting position.

Inverted Row

Inverted Rows typically are done in the rack or on a Smith machine. For variation, use straps or add resistance.

Starting Position and Movement

- Start with the bar 3 to 4 feet off the ground.
- Start in a supine position, arms fully extended, when you hold the bar (figure 8.23a).
- The bar should be high enough that your back is not touching the ground.
- Using a bench press grip, place your hands on the bar.
- Keeping your body rigid, pull your body up.

Upward and Downward Movements

- Pull your body up until your chest touches the bar (figure 8.23b). Hold this position for one to three seconds.
- Slowly lower your body to the starting position.

Figure 8.23   Inverted Row.

Hammer Back Machine

Procedure

- Adjust the seat and knee pad based on your height, setting your feet on the ground and grabbing the handles with the desired grip (overhand, underhand, or neutral).
- Actively pull the handles toward your chest and upper body by simultaneously retracting your scapulae and flexing your elbows.
- Bring the handles to your chest and upper body and then return to the starting position by protracting your scapulae and extending your elbows.

Iso Lateral Front Lat Pulldown

Procedure

- Grab the handles with the desired grip (overhand, underhand, or neutral).
- Pull the handles down to the lower portion of your chest.
- Return to the starting position.

Iso Lateral DY (Dorian Yates) Row

Procedure

- Grab the handles with the desired grip (overhand, underhand, or neutral).
- Pull the handles straight to the lower portion of your chest.
- Return to the starting position.

Iso High Row

Procedure

- Grab the handles with the desired grip (overhand or neutral).
- Pull the handles down to the higher portion of your chest.
- Return to the starting position.

Iso Lateral Low Row

Procedure

- Grab the handles with the desired grip (overhand or underhand).
- Pull the handles up to the lower portion of your chest.
- Return to the starting position.

Iso Row

Procedure

- Grab the handles with the desired grip (overhand, underhand, or neutral).
- Pull the handles straight to the middle portion of your chest.
- Return to the starting position.

SHOULDERS

Standing Shoulder Press

The Standing Shoulder Press develops the anterior and medial deltoids of the shoulders. You may perform this exercise using dumbbells or a barbell.

Starting Position

- Grasp the bar with a closed, pronated grip (figure 8.24a).
- Your grip should be slightly wider than shoulder width.
- Press the bar over your head until your elbows are fully extended (figure 8.24b).

Figure 8.24   Standing Shoulder Press.

(continued)

Downward Movement

- Inhale on the downward movement.
- Allow your elbows to slowly flex to lower the bar toward your head.
- Keep your wrists rigid and directly above your elbows.
- Extend your neck slightly to allow the bar to pass by your face (figure 8.24*c*) as it lowers to touch the clavicles and anterior deltoids.
- Maintain back and shoulder contact with the bench.

Upward Movement

- Exhale on the upward movement.
- Push the bar up until your elbows are fully extended.
- Extend your neck slightly to allow the bar to pass by your face as rises.
- Once the bar passes your head, bring your head back under so the bar is aligned with your ears.
- Keep your wrists rigid and directly above your elbows.
- Maintain your core position throughout the movement.

Figure 8.24 Standing Shoulder Press, *(continued)*.

Shoulder Circuit

The Shoulder Circuit is a supplemental exercise that isolates the deltoids and promotes muscle mass development through high volume. This circuit is a key component to increasing the integrity of the rotator cuff.

The circuit is made up of five exercises performed in a row with no rest except to change weight. Although the text here describes the exercises with dumbbells, you can use a barbell, cable machine, or exercise band. The first two exercises—Arnold Shoulder Press and Upright Row—are performed with heavier weight than the last three exercises—Front Shoulder Raise, Lateral Shoulder Raise, and Rear Shoulder Raise. Perform 6 repetitions of each exercise.

Arnold Shoulder Press

- Begin either sitting or standing.
- Maintain an upright posture while holding the dumbbells in a supinated position turned toward your body (figure 8.25a).
- Press and extend up while rotating the dumbbells out, finishing with the dumbbells turned away from your body (figure 8.25b).
- Once your arms are fully extended, lower the dumbbells under control back to the starting position.

Figure 8.25   Arnold Shoulder Press.

Upright Row

- Stand in an upright posture and hold the dumbbells just inside shoulder width (figure 8.26a).
- Pull the dumbbells up, finishing the movement when the dumbbells are directly underneath your chin (figure 8.26b).
- Lower the dumbbells to the starting position.

(continued)

Figure 8.26   Upright Row.

Front Shoulder Raise

- Stand upright with perfect posture (figure 8.27*a*). Hold the dumb-
  bells in either pronated or neutral grips.
- Raise the dumbbells to the front with both arms extended (figure
  8.27*b*).
- Stop the upward movement when the weight reaches eye level.
- Lower the weight under control back to the starting position.

Figure 8.27   Front Shoulder Raise.

Lateral Shoulder Raise

- Stand upright with your arms to your sides (figure 8.28a). Hold the dumbbells in either pronated or neutral grips.
- Raise the weight out away from your body (figure 8.28b).
- Finish the upward movement when the weight reaches eye level.
- Lower the weight under control back to the starting position.

Figure 8.28   Lateral Shoulder Raise.

Rear Shoulder Raise

- Stand in a bent-over position with your back parallel to the ground (figure 8.29a). Your hand position is neutral.
- Raise the weight out away from your body (figure 8.29b).
- Finish the upward movement when the weight reaches eye level.
- Lower the weight under control back to the starting position.

Figure 8.29   Rear Shoulder Raise.

Shoulder Combo

The Shoulder Combo circuit isolates the deltoids and promotes muscle mass development through high volume. This circuit is a key component to increasing the integrity of the rotator cuff.

The Shoulder Combo is made up of four exercises performed in a row with no rest except to change weight and dumbbells for the last exercise. The first three exercises—Front Shoulder Raise (page 164), Standing Shoulder Press (page 161), and Upright Row (page 163)—are performed with a barbell, and the last exercise—Rear Shoulder Raise (page 165—is performed using dumbbells. The repetitions are 6, 8, 8, and 10, respectively.

Three-Way Raise

The Three-Way Raise circuit is made up of three exercises performed in a row with dumbbells and no rest. Perform the Front Shoulder Raise (page 164), Lateral Shoulder Raise (page 165), and Rear Shoulder Raise (page 165) for 10 repetitions each.

Two-Way Raise

The Two-Way Raise is made up of two exercises performed in a row with dumbbells and no rest. Perform the Lateral Shoulder Raise and Rear Shoulder Raise (page 165) for 10 repetitions each.

Band Pull-Apart

Procedure

- Grip the ends of a jump-stretch band and straighten your arms.
- Raise the band until it is even with your shoulders.
- Pull the band apart until the band touches the midpoint of your chest, keeping your arms straight.
- Return to the starting position.

Face Pull

Equipment

- Cable attachment such as a triceps rope or cable handles
- Exercise band

Procedure

- Set the cable attachment or band at eye level or higher.
- Grab the cable attachment or band with an overhand grip, elbows in extension.
- Actively pull the cable attachment or band to your face.
- Keep your elbows above shoulder level.
- Return the cable attachment or band to the starting position in a controlled manner.

CHEST

Incline Bench Press

The Incline Bench Press strengthens the upper portions of the pectoralis major in the upper chest, the deltoids, and the triceps. This exercise can also be performed using two dumbbells and a closed, pronated grip.

Starting Position

- Do not use an incline of more than 45 degrees.
- Assume a supine position on the weight bench in a five-point body contact position.
- Grasp the bar with a closed, pronated grip.
- Place the bar over your chin with your elbows fully extended (figure 8.30*a*).
- Keep your back and glutes in full contact with the weight bench.

Downward Movement

- Inhale on the downward movement.
- Lower the bar to touch your upper chest just above midchest level (figure 8.30*b*).
- Keep your wrists rigid and directly above your elbows.
- Maintain the five-point body contact position.

Upward Movement

- Exhale through the sticking point of the upward movement.
- Push the bar up and slightly back until your elbows are fully extended.
- Keep your wrists rigid and directly above your elbows.
- Maintain the five-point body contact position. Do not arch your back or lift your butt off the bench.

Figure 8.30   Incline Bench Press.

Close Grip Bench Press

The Close Grip Bench Press develops the inner portion of the chest and the triceps.

Starting Position

- Assume a supine position on the weight bench in a five-point body contact position.
- Grasp the bar with a closed, pronated grip.
- Lie on the bench so that your eyes are below the edge of the supports.

Downward Movement

- Inhale on the downward movement.
- Lower the bar to touch your chest at approximately midchest level.
- Keep your elbows close to your sides. Do not flare them out to the sides.
- Keep your wrists rigid.
- Maintain the five-point body contact position.

Upward Movement

- Exhale through the sticking point of the upward movement.
- Push the bar up and slightly back. The bar should travel in a slight arc.
- Keep your wrists rigid and above your elbows.
- Maintain the five-point body contact position.

Dip

Procedure

- Use a dip rack or attachment.
- Start with your arms fully locked out (figure 8.31a).
- Bend at your elbows first and lower your body until your upper arms are parallel to the dip bar (figure 8.31b).
- Return to the starting position.

Figure 8.31   Dip.

Push-Up

Procedure

- Begin with your elbows in full extension, your hands spaced evenly apart, and your head in a neutral position.
- Simultaneously lower your entire body to the floor by flexing your elbows while keeping them in tight to your body.
- Simultaneously raise your entire body from the floor to the starting position by extending your elbows.

Horizontal Cable Press

Procedure

- Facing away from the cable machine, kneel on one knee.
- On the side of the down knee, reach back and grab the cable attachment handle.
- Pull the handle forward so the cable is under your armpit.
- Actively engage your core and the glute of your down leg and press forward.
- Extend your pressing arm to full extension without the shoulders rotating.
- Slowly allow the cable to retract while actively keeping your core engaged.

NECK

Four-Way Neck

Procedure

- Adjust the seat height on a neck machine so the pivot point lines up with the natural movement of your neck.
- Use the hand grips and keep your core tight.
- Perform flexion and extension to the front, back, left, and right sides (figure 8.32).

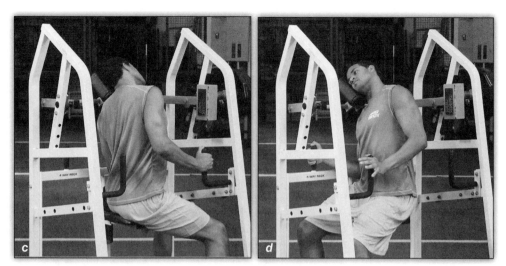

Figure 8.32   Four-Way Neck.

Six-Way Neck With Manual Resistance

This partner exercise uses the same movements as Four-Way Neck with two additional movements. You will perform flexion and extension to the front, back, left, and right sides. Also, you will perform two rotational movements: left and right.

Procedure

- Your partner stands behind you as you sit on a weight bench.
- Perform neck flexion and extension to the back, front, left, and right as your partner resists your movements eccentrically and concentrically (figure 8.33*a-d*).
- Your partner provides resistance by placing his hand on your head.
- Rotate your neck to the right and left as your partner resists your movements (figure 8.33*e-f*).
- After one full set, have your partner switch his hand to the left side of your jaw.
- When repetitions are completed, switch places with your partner.

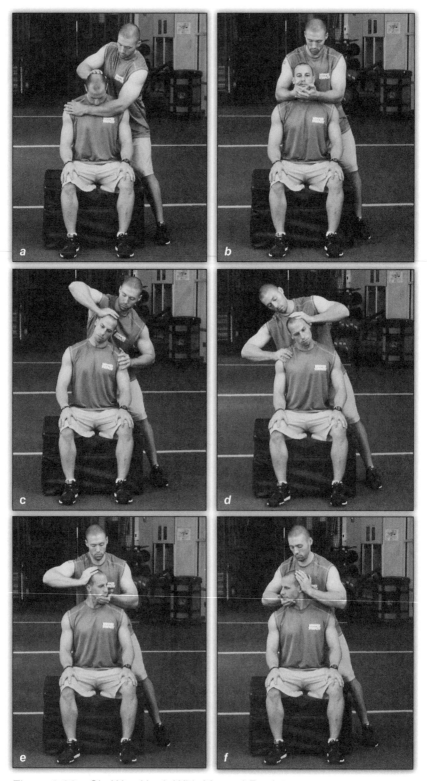

Figure 8.33 Six-Way Neck With Manual Resistance.

Neck Isolation

Train the front, back, and sides of your neck with manual resistance in an isometric fashion. You will need a partner and a stable surface.

Procedure

- Get into a six-point position on the floor with both feet, both knees, and both hands on the floor. Knees, hips, and shoulders are at 90-degree angles. Your partner stands at your head.
- Make sure your spine is in good alignment.
- Once you are in a good position, your partner applies pressure in all directions for 10 to 30 seconds. First, your partner places both hands on the back of your head and provides resistance. Second, your partner stands using both legs (quads) to provide resistance to the sides of your neck. Finally, your partner places both hands under your chin and provides resistance.

BICEPS

Biceps Curl

Procedure

- Hold a dumbbell in each hand. Stand with your arms hanging by your sides.
- Bend at your elbows to raise the dumbbells.
- Slowly lower the dumbbells to the starting position.

Weight Stack Curl

Use the weight stack to do double- or single-arm curls.

Procedure

- Stand facing the pulley machine.
- Grasp the bar attachment.
- Bend at your elbows and raise the bar attachment.
- Slowly lower the bar attachment to the starting position.

TRICEPS

Tate Press

Procedure

- Assume a supine position on a weight bench with your arms fully locked and your hands holding the dumbbells (figure 8.34*a*).
- Touch the insides of the dumbbells (figure 8.34*b*) and lower them to your chest while rotating so the insides touch your chest (figure 8.34*c*). Keep the dumbbells in contact throughout the movement.
- Keep your elbows at your sides while lowering and raising the dumbbells.

Figure 8.34
Tate Press.

Triceps Extension

Procedure

- Assume a supine position on a weight bench with your arms fully locked and your hands holding the dumbbells.
- Lower the weight while your elbows are pointed up.
- Only your elbow joints should move until the weight is close to the sides of your head. Return to the starting position.

Triceps Pushdown

Equipment

- Cable attachment
- Exercise band

Procedure

- Use an overhand or neutral grip, depending on the cable attachment or band, to grasp the attachment or band; elbows are bent at approximately 90 degrees.
- Actively extend your elbows to full extension.
- Return to the starting position in a controlled manner.

FOREARMS

Rice Bucket

Procedure

- Fill a 10-gallon bucket with rice.
- Insert your hands into the rice and use a squeezing motion to get to the bottom of the bucket.

Wrist Roller

Procedure

- Using a rope, attach a weight to a pipe.
- Wind the rope to raise and lower the weight by turning the pipe.

Sledgehammer

Procedure

- Grab the handle of a sledgehammer and raise and lower the end. Perform with the hammer end to the thumb side as well as the opposite.
- Vary the resistance by adjusting the distance of your hand from the weighted end.
- Also for variation, perform pronation and supination of the wrist. Imagine a windshield wiper.

CONCLUSION

Football is a total-body collision sport in which success depends on strength. Selecting the correct strength exercises can mean the difference between achieving your potential or not. The proper exercises not only help reduce injury, but also train you to be physically dominant.

Chapter 9

Conditioning

When training for anaerobic conditioning, use a 1:3 to 1:4 work-to-rest ratio. In the exercises described in this chapter, no specific work times are indicated to ensure that you use your own discretion based on your level of play. The ranges listed should be used for guidance only. Coaches should always consider the safety of the athletes first by making sure that sports medicine staff or other trained medical personnel are present with essential emergency equipment such as an AED machine and inhalers. Water breaks should be planned, and water kept readily available at all times.

The coach's role in conditioning is to properly plan and supervise the workouts. To do this, the coach must address variables such as the current conditioning level of the team, training cycle, the size of the facilities, the number of staff members available to execute the plan, weather conditions, and the availability of emergency services. A well-planned and well-executed program will prepare athletes for the rigors of the game.

The following equipment is needed for the exercises described in this chapter:

- Cones
- Stopwatches
- Whistles
- Clipboards, daily training plans, pencils
- Bullhorn (if necessary)

Play Drives

Play Drives enhance metabolic conditioning of the lactic acid (LA) system. Play Drives elicit a physiological response similar to a drive in a game. Each drive has 12 plays that must be run at full speed to designated distances. There is a 25-second rest period between plays and a 3-minute rest between quarters.

A lined football field and stopwatch are needed. Use the drill card that applies to each position (tables 9.1 through 9.4). Carry your position card when running if a coach is not present. On the card, the numbering

Table 9.1   Drill Card for Offensive Line

Play	Field	Go/Stop	Time (sec.)	Yards
1	+G:36	0:00 to 0:08	8	64
2	−40:11	0:33 to 0:39	6	49
3	+G:34	1:04 to 1:08	4	34
4	+30:47	1:33 to 1:35	2	17
5	−50:01	2:00 to 2:06	6	49
6	+G:17	2:31 to 2:33	2	17
7	+20:46	2:58 to 3:02	4	34
8	−50:01	3:27 to 3:33	6	49
9	+G:36	3:58 to 4:06	8	64
10	−40:26	4:31 to 4:35	4	34
11	+25:42	5:00 to 5:02	2	17
12	−49:G	5:27 to 5:33	6	49

Table 9.2   Drill Card for Defensive Line and Ends

Play	Field	Go/Stop	Time (sec.)	Yards
1	+G:32	0:00 to 0:08	8	68
2	−40:07	0:33 to 0:39	6	53
3	+10:46	1:04 to 1:08	4	36
4	−40:21	1:33 to 1:35	2	19
5	+10:37	2:00 to 2:06	6	53
6	−30:49	2:31 to 2:33	2	19
7	−50:14	2:58 to 3:02	4	36
8	+05:42	3:27 to 3:33	6	53
9	−32:G	3:58 to 4:06	8	68
10	+G:36	4:31 to 4:35	4	36
11	+30:49	5:00 to 5:02	2	19
12	−47:G	5:27 to 5:33	6	53

under the Field column designates the yard line and direction in which to run. All quarters begin on the goal line (G). A plus sign (+) means to run away from the starting goal line. A minus sign (–) means to run toward the starting goal line. The first number represents the yard line or goal line to begin each play from. The second number indicates the yard line to finish each play on. Underlined numbers (e.g., –25:40) designate yard lines across midfield from the starting goal line.

Table 9.3 Drill Card for Linebackers, Tight Ends, Quarterbacks, Kickers, and Punters

Play	Field	Go/Stop	Time (sec.)	Yards
1	+G:29	0:00 to 0:08	8	71
2	–30:16	0:33 to 0:39	6	54
3	+10:47	1:04 to 1:08	4	37
4	–50:31	1:33 to 1:35	2	19
5	+20:26	2:00 to 2:06	6	54
6	–30:49	2:31 to 2:33	2	19
7	–40:03	2:58 to 3:02	4	37
8	+10:36	3:27 to 3:33	6	49
9	–29:G	3:58 to 4:06	8	71
10	+G:37	4:31 to 4:35	4	37
11	+30:49	5:00 to 5:02	2	19
12	–45:01	5:27 to 5:33	6	54

Table 9.4 Drill Card for Receivers, Running Backs, and Defensive Backs

Play	Field	Go/Stop	Time (sec.)	Yards
1	+G:27	0:00 to 0:08	8	73
2	–30:14	0:33 to 0:39	6	56
3	+G:39	1:04 to 1:08	4	39
4	+40:40	1:33 to 1:35	2	20
5	–40:04	2:00 to 2:06	6	56
6	+G:20	2:31 to 2:33	2	20
7	+20:41	2:58 to 3:02	4	39
8	–40:04	3:27 to 3:33	6	56
9	+G:27	3:58 to 4:06	8	73
10	–30:31	4:31 to 4:35	4	39
11	+30:50	5:00 to 5:02	2	20
12	–40:04	5:27 to 5:33	6	56

Start the first sprint and stopwatch together, and allow the stopwatch to run continuously. Start and stop each run on the yard lines indicated. The 25-second rest period is built into the times. Walk to the next yard line and begin when indicated. The times and yards of each sprint are given as well. At the completion of each quarter, stop the watch, begin your 3-minute rest, and return to the goal line. Reset the stopwatch to zero and begin the next quarter.

Half Gassers (106s)

Start on the sideline of the football field in a three-point stance with your hand behind the sideline. The coach will blow a whistle to begin the run. Run to the opposite sideline, touch on or over the line, and run back, a distance of 106 yards, within the time designated for your position. Once the designated time has expired, rest for 45 to 60 seconds before taking your three-point stance to begin the next run. The coach will blow the whistle to begin the next rep of the drill.

Time Ranges

Offensive linemen: 19 to 22 seconds

Defensive linemen, kickers, punters: 18 to 21 seconds

Linebackers, tight ends: 16 to 19 seconds

Quarterbacks, running backs, wide receivers, defensive backs: 15 to 17 seconds

Suicide Gassers

As with all gassers, you begin on the sideline. First, run to the near hash mark and back to the sideline. Next, run to the far hash mark and back to the original sideline. Finally, run across the field to the opposite sideline and back.

350s

Start on the corner of the football field. Run one lap around the field in the time prescribed for your position. Rest three to four minutes between runs.

Time Ranges

Offensive linemen: 72 to 77 seconds

Defensive tackles: 70 to 75 seconds

Defensive ends, tight ends: 68 to 73 seconds

Linebackers, kickers, punters: 64 to 69 seconds

Safeties, running backs: 61 to 66 seconds

Cornerbacks, quarterbacks, wide receivers: 58 to 63 seconds

110s (Conditioning or Testing)

Start on the end line of the football field, the line the goalpost is on. Begin on the end line in a three-point stance with your hand behind the line. The coach blows the whistle to begin the run. Run to the opposite goal line, a distance of 110 yards, within the time designated for your position. Once the designated time has expired, a 45- to 60-second rest period begins before you begin the next run. For example, the rest time for a linebacker will begin at 18 seconds even if he takes more time than that to finish the run. If you are not ready to begin the run in time, you must wait until the next repetition to run and complete any missed runs after the prescribed number of repetitions are complete. The coach will blow the whistle to begin the next repetition of the drill.

Time Ranges

Offensive linemen: 19 to 21 seconds

Defensive linemen, kickers, punters: 18 to 20 seconds

Linebackers, tight ends: 16 to 18 seconds

Quarterbacks, running backs, wide receivers, defensive backs: 15 to 17 seconds

300-Yard Shuttle

Start at the goal line of the football field. Sprint to the 25-yard line and return to the starting goal line for six round trips (12 × 25 yards = 300 yards). Complete the drill within the prescribed time range for your position, taking a two- to three-minute rest between runs.

Time Ranges

Offensive linemen: 65 to 75 seconds

Defensive linemen, kickers, punters: 60 to 70 seconds

Linebackers, tight ends: 55 to 65 seconds

Running backs, wide receivers, defensive backs, quarterbacks: 50 to 60 seconds

Power Training (PTs)

The offensive linemen, tight ends, running backs, and wide receivers make up group 1. They start at designated corners on the goal line of the end zone (figure 9.1). The defensive linemen, kickers, punters, linebackers, quarterbacks, and defensive backs make up group 2. While group 1 is performing the drill, group 2 either rests or performs specified circuit exercises such as push-ups or sit-ups. The coach raises a hand to signal both groups to take their marks. When the coach blows the whistle, the players in group 1 run one full lap either counterclockwise or clockwise (as designated by the coach) around the cones and finish in the same area in which they started. Players in group 2 perform their circuit work. All players performing the run start at the front cone and finish at the back cone. Once group 1 finishes the run, the coach raises a hand to signal both groups to get in position for the rest interval. During the rest interval, both groups perform 20 crunches or push-ups and then return to the standing position to wait for the next repetition. The rest intervals for each group last as long as it takes for the other group to complete the run (1:1 work to rest). For the next repetition, group 1 performs the circuit exercises and group 2 runs.

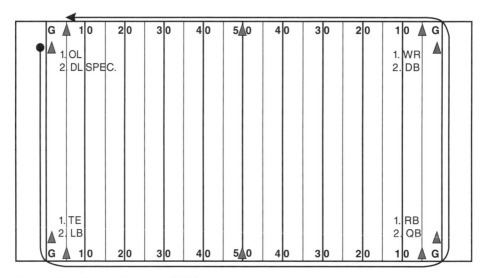

Figure 9.1   Power Training (PTs).

Time Ranges

Offensive linemen: 65 to 75 seconds

Defensive linemen, kickers, punters: 60 to 70 seconds

Linebackers, tight ends: 55 to 65 seconds

Running backs, wide receivers, defensive backs, quarterbacks: 50 to 60 seconds

Full Gassers (212s)

Start at the sideline of the football field. Run from the beginning sideline to the opposite sideline, return to the beginning sideline, and repeat for a total of 212 yards.

Time Ranges

Offensive linemen: 43 to 48 seconds

Defensive tackles: 40 to 45 seconds

Defensive ends, linebackers, tight ends, kickers, punters: 37 to 43 seconds

Wide receivers, defensive backs, running backs, quarterbacks: 34 to 39 seconds

Tempo Runs

For the first set (figure 9.2a), start on the goal line and sprint 100 yards. Walk to the 25-yard line and back to the goal line, a total of 50 yards, to recover. Start on the goal line and sprint another 100 yards (figure 9.2b).

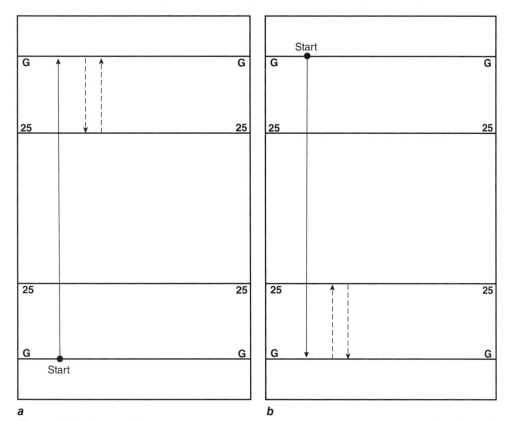

a   *b*

Figure 9.2 Tempo Runs.   *(continued)*

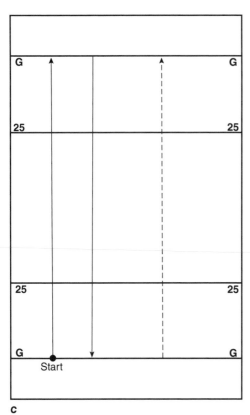

c

Figure 9.2 Tempo Runs, *continued.*

Walk to the 25-yard line and back to the goal line to recover. Start on the goal line and sprint 200 yards, running down to the opposite goal line and back (figure 9.2c). Walk 100 yards for recovery. This is considered one set.

For the second set, sprint 100 yards with a recovery walk to the 25-yard line and back, sprint 200 yards with a recovery walk to the 25-yard line and back, and sprint 100 yards with a 100-yard recovery walk.

For the third set, sprint 200 yards with a recovery walk to the 25-yard line and back, sprint 100 yards with a recovery walk to the 25-yard line and back, and sprint 100 yards with a 100-yard recovery walk.

For the fourth set, repeat the sequence and yardage of the first set. You must meet or beat the prescribed running times.

Time Ranges

Offensive linemen, defensive tackles: 18 to 20 seconds for 100 yards, 38 to 42 seconds for 200 yards

Defensive ends, linebackers, tight ends, kickers, punters: 16 to 18 seconds for 100 yards, 34 to 38 seconds for 200 yards

Wide receivers, defensive backs, running backs, quarterbacks: 14 to 16 seconds for 100 yards, 30 to 34 seconds for 200 yards

Stadium Stair Running

When performed using a longer work-to-rest ratio, stair running builds strength for sprinting. It is a great conditioning tool when done using a shorter work-to-rest ratio. Because of the many stadium configurations, there are no hard rules. To build sprint power specifically, allow for nearly a full recovery (1:5 work-to-rest ratio or greater depending on your conditioning level). To use stadium stair running as a conditioning drill, decrease rest times to achieve a 1:3 work-to-rest ratio or less.

Options

- Run every step to the top.
- Run every other step to the top.
- Run laterally every step or every other step to the top.
- Run laterally with a crossover step to the top.
- Perform double-leg hops by jumping off both feet, covering as many steps as possible for a prescribed number of repetitions. Your goal is to cover as much ground as possible within the repetitions.
- Perform single-leg hops in the same way as the double-leg hops except jump off the right and left legs independently.
- Continuously run up and back. Run up one set of stairs and walk back briskly. Repeat immediately after reaching the bottom of the steps. (If you are running in a group, you will need to walk down the bleacher seats to avoid colliding with the other runners.)
- Perform snake runs. Run up one set of stairs, jog across to the next set, and briskly walk or jog to the bottom. Jog across to the next set and return to the top. Repeat for a prescribed number of runs to the top.

Hill Running

Hill Running is similar to Stadium Stair Run (see chapter 5, page 83). Because hills vary in length and incline, the only rule of thumb is the work-to-rest ratios. To build sprint power, keep runs to 10 seconds or less with full recovery (1:5 work-to-rest ratio or greater depending on conditioning). For a conditioning effect, reduce the ratio to 1:3 or less or increase the length of the run.

Cardio Machine Drills

Cardio machines are an option when a running surface is not available or extra work with no impact is desired. Interval sprints on a machine are most applicable to the football player. When doing interval sprints, use a high-speed rpm for the work portion and a low-speed rpm for the rest portion. Typically, machines such as the elliptical trainer and stationary bike are used. If you use a treadmill, stand on the sides of the treadmill off the belt to rest while the treadmill continues to run. Use a work-to-rest ratio in the 1:3 range for a conditioning effect. Continuous work is more for aerobic conditioning, which may be valuable if you are recovering from injury or need to improve your body composition.

CONCLUSION

Various cardiorespiratory conditioning options are available, which is fortunate because football players require a wide range of options to build endurance. Those with optimal endurance can play at a high level for four quarters and overtime, if necessary.

Part III

TRAINING SCHEDULE AND WORKOUTS

Chapter 10

Off-Season Workouts

When designing a training program, coaches and athletes must take all aspects of the athlete's training into consideration. Results are the most important goal and the factor by which a program is ultimately measured. Every program is unique because desired results vary.

Many variables and philosophies drive program design. To help you achieve the best results over time, your program should be progressive while appropriately addressing all of your strengths and weaknesses. A progressive approach helps you avoid plateaus, thereby preventing stagnation in your athletic development.

Understanding the big picture is paramount when designing a program. Program design should be looked at several times a year, not just once a year, over several years. When designing a program, consider many factors such as the number of training days during a week, the total number of weeks (microcycle), the total training session time, off days, and active rest.

OFF-SEASON DEVELOPMENTAL TRAINING

During the off-season, lifting is done during three total-body strength training sessions per week (Monday, Wednesday, and Friday). Each session begins with a dynamic warm-up and stretch routine followed by core stabilization (team abs; see chapter 4). The first portion of the lifting workout begins with the core lift of the day—Hang Clean, Bench Press, Back Squat, or a variation depending on level assignments. After you have completed the core lift, begin the auxiliary and supplemental exercises. Supplemental exercises address your particular weaknesses and needs. The final portion of the workout consists of hip mobility and cool-down stretches. Off-season testing is conducted during the final week.

Running consists of anaerobic conditioning to prepare the team for Mat Drills (page 92). Mat Drills are conducted on Tuesday and Thursday mornings with performance testing on Friday afternoons. Mat Drills are short agility and acceleration–based movements performed on a wrestling mat or a 15-x-15-foot area. (See chapter 6.)

MULTILEVEL PROGRAM PROGRESSION

All athletes entering the program begin at level zero. During the winter semester, level zero training usually lasts four to six weeks followed by testing before athletes begin level one. Level one training takes place during and after spring football. All winter level-one athletes are promoted to level two for the summer.

The basic requirement for promotion from level two to three is being strong enough to play the position. Positional standards instituted as benchmarks are used to determine if athletes are strong enough to move to level three. (See chapter 2, page 17.) To be considered for promotion, an athlete must typically attain two of the four strength standards (one being for the Back Squat), one of the two explosive jump standards, and one of the two agility standards. Another factor considered is whether more explosive-type training would be beneficial in developing overall athleticism. (See the goals for level three on page 11.)

The basic requirement for promotion from level two to level three is having enough relative strength to play the position. However body composition is a very important factor in promotion from level three to level four. Level four requires more ability to produce and absorb force. Not all athletes will reach level four.

INTANGIBLE BENCHMARKS

- To progress from level two to level three, you must be a self-starter, be trustworthy, and possess a positive mental attitude.
- To progress from level three to level four, you must be a leader and a role model, be confident, and be focused.

TRAINING TEMPO IN THE WEIGHT ROOM

The off-season training tempo allows for near total recovery between the core lifts and auxiliary strength-based exercises. As the training cycle approaches the designated testing period, you are allowed to sit between sets for faster recovery. This tempo permits maximal strength gains. Once you have completed all strength and power–based exercises, you should try to increase your training tempo until completion of the workout.

AUTOREGULATORY PROGRESSIVE RESISTANCE EXERCISE (APRE)

APRE is a training method based on what a person can accomplish for that day of training. With percentage-based progression models, the weights are rigid and adjustments are sometimes problematic when setbacks occur such as minor injuries or not achieving the prescribed repetitions. The APRE model is adjustable within and between workouts. These are the benefits of APRE training:

- Creates rapid strength gains
- Allows the athlete to progress at his own rate
- Is significantly better than linear periodization in periods of less than 12 weeks
- Features a variety of protocols to develop various strengths and traits

The three protocols are APRE3, APRE6, and APRE10. Choosing the most appropriate protocol depends on what type of strength you're trying to develop. The APRE3 is based on an estimated 3-rep max (3RM) and is used for developing maximum strength and power. The APRE6 is based on an estimated 6RM and is used for developing strength and hypertrophy. The APRE10 is based on an estimated 10RM and is used for hypertrophy.

As you can see from table 10.1, the setup is the same for each of the routines: a light set of 50 percent of the RM followed by a second set with 75 percent of the RM, and a third set with maximum repetitions at the RM. The fourth and final sets are adjusted based on the repetitions attained during the third set (table 10.2). They are performed to maximum repetitions again, which determines the RM for the following week.

As an example, use the 3RM routine for an athlete with an estimated 3RM of 300 pounds on the Bench Press. The athlete warms up for his first set with 150 pounds for 6 repetitions (150 pounds is 50 percent of 300 pounds). He then completes a set of 3 repetitions with 225 pounds (225 pounds is 75 percent of 300 pounds). The assigned weight for the third set is 300 pounds, which is the estimated 3RM, and the athlete does maximum repetitions.

Table 10.1 Autoregulatory Progressive Resistance Exercise (APRE) Routines

Set	APRE3 (3RM)	APRE6 (6RM)	APRE10 (10RM)
0	Warm-up	Warm-up	Warm-up
1	6 reps at 50% 3RM	10 reps at 50% 6RM	12 reps at 50% 10RM
2	3 reps at 75% 3RM	6 reps at 75% 6RM	10 reps at 75% 10RM
3	Reps to failure at 3RM	Reps to failure at 6RM	Reps to failure at 10RM
4	Adjusted reps to failure	Adjusted reps to failure	Adjusted reps to failure

Table 10.2 Adjustment Table for APRE

APRE3 (3RM)		APRE6 (6RM)		APRE10 (10RM)	
Repetitions	**Set 4**	**Repetitions**	**Set 4**	**Repetitions**	**Set 4**
1 or 2	Decrease 5 to 10	0 to 2	Decrease 5 to 10	4 to 6	Decrease 5 to 10
3 or 4	Same	3 or 4	Decrease 0 to 5	7 or 8	Decrease 0 to 5
5 or 6	Increase 5 to 10	5 to 7	Same	9 to 11	Same
7 and up	Increase 10 to 15	8 to 12	Increase 5 to 10	12 to 16	Increase 5 to 10
		13 and up	Increase 10 to 15	17 and up	Increase 10 to 15

In this case the athlete completes 7 repetitions. Using the APRE adjustment chart, find the number of repetitions performed under the 3RM routine in the left-hand column, which in this case is 7. In the right-hand column, across from this, we see that the athlete should increase the weight by 10 to 15 pounds. For set 4, the athlete performs repetitions with 315 pounds. The athlete successfully performs 6 repetitions on set 4. Referring to the adjustment chart, we see that 6 repetitions is an increase of 5 to 10 pounds, which changes the estimated 3RM to 320 to 325 pounds. This will then be the weight the athlete will use for the next Bench Press training day.

Any of the protocols can be used this way. The number of repetitions completed in the third set determines the weight used in the fourth set, and the number of repetitions completed in the fourth set determines the weight used in the third set the following week.

TRAINING PROGRAMS

The off-season training programs (tables 10.3 through 10.13) are based on the multilevel system introduced in chapter 1 (page 9). This comprehensive period of training is critical for the total development of athleticism. It is important to understand that multisport athletes, such as those at the high school level, may require reductions in volume (sets and reps) to reduce the possibility of overtraining. The off-season should focus on building power and strength to new PR levels in preparation for the next competition season.

Prelift Activity

1. Dynamic warm-up
2. Stretch
3. Core
4. Rotator Cuff and Scap Circuit

Table 10.3 Off-Season Workout Level Zero

Workout 1								
Body weight circuit	**Reps**	**Date**	**Reps**	**Date**	**Reps**	**Date**	**Reps**	**Date**
Body Weight Squat	2 × 20							
Push-Up	2 × 20							
Split Squat	2 × 20							
Team circuit*	**Reps**	**Date**	**Reps**	**Date**	**Reps**	**Date**	**Reps**	**Date**
Medicine Ball Chest Pass								
Plate Push								
Overhead Stair Walk								
Walking Lunge								
Ab exercise of choice								
Workout 2								
Body weight circuit	**Reps**	**Date**	**Reps**	**Date**	**Reps**	**Date**	**Reps**	**Date**
Split Jump	2 × 20							
Plate Push	6 × 15 yards							
Pull-Up	20							
Team circuit*	**Reps**	**Date**	**Reps**	**Date**	**Reps**	**Date**	**Reps**	**Date**
Front Bear Crawl								
Push-Up								
Walking Lunge								
Squat Jump								
Ab exercise of choice								
Workout 3								
Body weight circuit	**Reps**	**Date**	**Reps**	**Date**	**Reps**	**Date**	**Reps**	**Date**
Push-Up	2 × 20							
Body Weight Squat	2 × 20							
Inverted Row	2 × 20							
Team circuit*	**Reps**	**Date**	**Reps**	**Date**	**Reps**	**Date**	**Reps**	**Date**
Spiderman								
Walking Lunge								
Lateral Walking Lunge								
Squat Jump								
Ab exercise of choice								

*Perform team circuits as a team with set parameters for successful completion together. Before the exercise starts, the coach determines the number of repetitions. Everyone counts the repetitions. Effort level must be high for all players, with no one missing a repetition. Follow instructions as given for the exercise to be performed.

Table 10.4　Off-Season Workout Level One

Monday	Reps	Date	Reps	Date	Reps	Date	Reps	Date
Back Squat	10							
APRE6	6							
	M							
	M							
Barbell Row	10							
	10							
	10							
Biceps Curl	10							
	10							
	10							
Six-Way Neck With Manual Resistance	10							
	10							
Wednesday	Reps	Date	Reps	Date	Reps	Date	Reps	Date
Bench Press	10							
APRE6	6							
	M							
	M							
Romanian Dead Lift (RDL)	10							
	10							
	10							
Pistol Squat	8							
	8							
	8							
Hammer Back Machine	8							
	8							
	8							
Triceps Extension	10							
	10							
	10							

Friday								
	Reps	**Date**	**Reps**	**Date**	**Reps**	**Date**	**Reps**	**Date**
Hang Clean Complex Technique (Power Shrug × 3, High Pull × 2, Hang Clean × 1)	2 sets							
Hang Clean	5							
	5							
	5							
225 Reps (test)	1 set							
Max Pull-Up (test)	1 set							
Ab Circuit	2 sets							
Four-Way Neck	1 × 10							

M = maximum repetitions (as many reps as possible)

Table 10.5   Off-Season Workout Level Two, Phase One

Monday								
	Reps	**Date**	**Reps**	**Date**	**Reps**	**Date**	**Reps**	**Date**
Back Squat	10							
APRE6	6							
	M							
	M							
Standing Shoulder Press	8							
	8							
	8							
Barbell Row	8							
	8							
	8							
Push/Pull Circuit	5 each							
	5 each							
	5 each							
Pistol Squat	8							
	8							
	8							
Glute Ham Raise	8							
	8							
	8							

(continued)

Table 10.5, *continued*

Wednesday								
	Reps	**Date**	**Reps**	**Date**	**Reps**	**Date**	**Reps**	**Date**
Hang Clean	4							
	4							
	4							
	4							
Bench Press	10							
APRE6	6							
	M							
	M							
Romanian Dead Lift	10							
	10							
	10							
Triceps Pushdown	1 min.							
Shoulder Combo 6-8-8-10	2 sets							
One-Arm Dumbbell Row	8							
	8							
	8							
Friday								
	Reps	**Date**	**Reps**	**Date**	**Reps**	**Date**	**Reps**	**Date**
225 Reps (test)								
Front Squat	6							
	6							
	6							
Pull-Up	M							
	M							
	M							
Two-Way Raise (lateral, rear)	2 sets							
Ab Circuit	3 sets							
Reverse Walking Lunge	2 × 10							
	2 × 10							

M = maximum repetitions (as many reps as possible)

Table 10.6 Off-Season Workout Level Two, Phase Two

Monday	Reps	Date	Reps	Date	Reps	Date	Reps	Date
Back Squat	5							
	3							
	3							
	3							
	5							
Standing Shoulder Press	6							
	6							
	6							
Pull-Up	M							
	M							
	M							
Pistol Squat	8							
	8							
	8							
Push/Pull Circuit	5							
	5							
	5							
Glute Ham Raise	8							
	8							
	8							
Wednesday	Reps	Date	Reps	Date	Reps	Date	Reps	Date
Bench Press	5							
	3							
	3							
	3							
	5							
Hang Clean	3							
	3							
	3							
	3							
	5							

(continued)

Table 10.6, *continued*

Wednesday *(continued)*								
	Reps	**Date**	**Reps**	**Date**	**Reps**	**Date**	**Reps**	**Date**
Romanian Dead Lift (RDL)	8							
	8							
	8							
Triceps Pushdown	1 min.							
Shoulder Circuit with dumbbells 6-6-6-6-6	2 sets							
One-Arm Dumbbell Row	6							
	6							
	6							
Friday								
	Reps	**Date**	**Reps**	**Date**	**Reps**	**Date**	**Reps**	**Date**
225 Reps (test)								
Plate Push (45 pounds)	5 × 20 yd.							
Reverse Hyperextension	10							
	10							
Cuban Press	10							
	10							
Hammer Back Machine	8							
	8							
	8							
Four-Way Neck	10							
Ab Circuit	3 sets							
Walking Lunge	10							
	10							

M = maximum repetitions (as many reps as possible)

Table 10.7   Off-Season Workout Level Two, Phase Three

Monday	Reps	Date	Reps	Date	Reps	Date	Reps	Date
5-Repetition Back Squat Max Test	3							
	3							
	1							
	1							
	5							
Hammer Back Machine	8							
	8							
	8							
Push/Pull Circuit	5							
	5							
	5							
Biceps Curl	10							
	10							
	10							
Pistol Squat	8							
	8							
	8							
Height and Weight (test)								
Wednesday	**Reps**	**Date**	**Reps**	**Date**	**Reps**	**Date**	**Reps**	**Date**
225 Reps (test)*								
Three-Way Raise	3 sets							
Triceps Extension	10							
	10							
	10							
5-Repetition Bench Max Test*	3							
	3							
	1							
	1							
	5							
Hammer Back Machine	8							
	8							
	8							

(continued)

Table 10.7, *continued*

Friday	Reps	Date	Reps	Date	Reps	Date	Reps	Date
5-Repetition Hang Clean Max Test	3							
	3							
	1							
	1							
	5							
Hip and Groin Flexibility Test (V-Sit, Sit and Reach)								
Max Pull-Up Test								
Four-Way Neck	2 × 10							
Ab Circuit	3 sets							
All retests completed								

M = maximum repetitions (as many reps as possible)
The 225 Reps and 5-Repetition Max tests should be done on different weeks.

Table 10.8 Off-Season Workout Level Three, Phase One

Monday	Reps	Date	Reps	Date	Reps	Date	Reps	Date
Back Squat	5							
	3							
	3							
	3							
	5							
Standing Shoulder Press	8							
	8							
	8							
Push/Pull Circuit	5							
	5							
	5							
Pistol Squat	8							
	8							
	8							
Barbell Row	8							
	8							
	8							
Glute Ham Raise	8							
	8							
	8							

Wednesday								
	Reps	**Date**	**Reps**	**Date**	**Reps**	**Date**	**Reps**	**Date**
Bench Press	8							
	5							
	3							
	3							
	M							
Hang Clean (Tendo at 1.55 m/s)	3							
	3							
	3							
	3							
	3							
Split Squat	8							
	8							
Shoulder Combo 6-8-8-10	2 sets							
One-Arm Dumbbell Row	8							
	8							
	8							
Romanian Dead Lift (RDL)	10							
	10							
	10							
Friday								
	Reps	**Date**	**Reps**	**Date**	**Reps**	**Date**	**Reps**	**Date**
225 Reps (practice)	M							
Sled Pull (use heavy weight and walk; do not run)	4 × 20 yd.							
Pull-Up	M							
	M							
	M							
Two-Way Raise (lateral, rear)	2 sets							
Ab Circuit	3 sets							

M = maximum repetitions (as many reps as possible)

Table 10.9 Off-Season Workout Level Three, Phase Two

Monday	Reps	Date	Reps	Date	Reps	Date	Reps	Date
Back Squat	5							
	3							
	1							
	1							
	5							
Standing Shoulder Press	6							
	6							
	6							
Push/Pull Circuit	5							
	5							
	5							
Pistol Squat	6							
	6							
	6							
Pull-Up	M							
	M							
	M							
Glute Ham Raise	8							
	8							
	8							

Wednesday	Reps	Date	Reps	Date	Reps	Date	Reps	Date
Bench Press	8							
	5							
	5							
	5							
	M							
Triceps Pushdown	1 min.							
Hang Clean (Tendo at 1.55 m/s)	3							
	3							
	3							
	3							
	3							
Split Squat	8							
	8							

Wednesday *(continued)*								
	Reps	**Date**	**Reps**	**Date**	**Reps**	**Date**	**Reps**	**Date**
Shoulder Circuit with dumbbells 6-6-6-6-6	2 sets							
One-Arm Dumbbell Row (heavy)	6							
	6							
	6							
Romanian Dead Lift (RDL)	8							
	8							
	8							
Friday								
	Reps	**Date**	**Reps**	**Date**	**Reps**	**Date**	**Reps**	**Date**
225 Reps (test)	M							
Dip	15							
	15							
Sled Pull, four-plate minimum (use heavy weight and walk; do not run)	5 × 20 yd.							
Reverse Hyperextension	10							
	10							
Hammer Back Machine	8							
	8							
	8							
Cuban Press	10							
	10							
Four-Way Neck	10							
Ab Circuit	3 sets							

M = maximum repetitions (as many reps as possible)

Table 10.10 Off-Season Workout Level Three, Phase Three

Monday	Reps	Date	Reps	Date	Reps	Date	Reps	Date
5-Repetition Back Squat Max Test	3							
	3							
	1							
	1							
	5							
Hammer Back Machine	8							
	8							
	8							
Push/Pull Circuit	5							
	5							
	5							
Biceps Curl	10							
	10							
	10							
Pistol Squat	8							
	8							
	8							
Height and Weight (test)								

Wednesday	Reps	Date	Reps	Date	Reps	Date	Reps	Date
5-Repetition Bench Max Test	3							
	3							
	1							
	1							
	5							
Three-Way Raise (front, lateral, rear)	3 sets							
Tate Press	10							
	10							
	10							
Hammer Back Machine	8							
	8							
	8							

Friday								
	Reps	**Date**	**Reps**	**Date**	**Reps**	**Date**	**Reps**	**Date**
3-Repetition Speed Clean Max Test	3							
	3							
	3							
	3							
	3							
225 Reps (test)	M							
Hip and Groin Flexibility Test (V-Sit, Sit and Reach)								
Max Pull-Up Test								
Four-Way Neck	2 × 10							
Ab Circuit	3 sets							
All retests completed								

M = maximum repetitions (as many reps as possible)

Table 10.11   Off-Season Workout Level Four, Phase One

Monday								
	Reps	**Date**	**Reps**	**Date**	**Reps**	**Date**	**Reps**	**Date**
Box Squat (Tendo at 0.8m/s)	2							
	2							
	2							
	2							
	2							
Box Jump (OL and DL)	3 × 3							
Box Jump (QB, RB, WR, TE, LB, DB, K, P)	4 × 3							
Standing Shoulder Press	8							
	8							
	8							
Barbell Row	8							
	8							
	8							
Glute Ham Raise	8							
	8							
	8							

(continued)

Table 10.11, *continued*

Wednesday								
	Reps	**Date**	**Reps**	**Date**	**Reps**	**Date**	**Reps**	**Date**
Board Bench Press (with chains, two or three boards)	3							
	3							
	3							
	3							
	3							
	3							
Triceps Pushdown	1 min.							
Hang Clean (Tendo at 1.55m/s)	2							
	2							
	2							
	2							
	2							
	2							
Shoulder Combo 6-8-8-10	1 set							
Romanian Dead Lift (RDL) (heavy)	8							
	8							
	8							
Friday								
	Reps	**Date**	**Reps**	**Date**	**Reps**	**Date**	**Reps**	**Date**
225 Reps								
Dip (QB, RB, WR, TE, LB, DB, K, P: weighted)	20							
Sled Pull (heavy weight and walk; do not run)	4 × 20 yd.							
Pull-Up	3 sets							
OL and DL: eccentric × 6 (4 sec.)								
QB, RB, WR, TE, LB, DB, K, P: use weight × M								
Split Squat	8							
	8							
Two-Way Raise (lateral, rear)	2 sets							
Ab Circuit	3 sets							

M = maximum repetitions (as many reps as possible)

Table 10.12 Off-Season Workout Level Four, Phase Two

Monday	Reps	Date	Reps	Date	Reps	Date	Reps	Date
Back Squat	5							
	3							
	1							
	1							
	5							
Box Jump (OL and DL) Skill 4 × 3	3 × 3							
Box Jump (QB, RB, WR, TE, LB, DB, K, P)	4 × 3							
Standing Shoulder Press	6							
	6							
	6							
Pull-Up	3 sets							
OL and DL: eccentric × 6 (4 sec.)								
QB, RB, WR, TE, LB, DB, K, P: use weight × M								
Glute Ham Raise (weighted)	8							
	8							
Wednesday	Reps	Date	Reps	Date	Reps	Date	Reps	Date
Bench Press	3							
	3							
	2							
	1							
	1							
	1							
Triceps Pushdown	1 min.							
Hang Clean (Tendo at 1.55m/s)	1							
	1							
	1							
	1							

(continued)

Table 10.12, *continued*

Wednesday *(continued)*								
	Reps	**Date**	**Reps**	**Date**	**Reps**	**Date**	**Reps**	**Date**
Split Squat	8							
	8							
Shoulder Circuit with dumbbells 6-6-6-6-6	1 set							
Romanian Dead Lift (RDL) (feet 36 inches apart)	6							
	6							
	6							
Friday								
		Date	Reps	Date	Reps	Date	Reps	Date
225 Reps	M							
Dip (QB, RB, WR, TE, LB, DB, K, P: weighted)	20							
Sled Pull (heavy weight and walk; do not run)	5 × 20 yd.							
Reverse Hyperextension	10							
	10							
Hammer Back Machine	8							
	8							
	8							
Cuban Press	10							
	10							
Four-Way Neck	10							
Ab Circuit	1 set							

M = maximum repetitions (as many reps as possible)

Table 10.13 Off-Season Workout Level Four, Phase Three

Monday	Reps	Date	Reps	Date	Reps	Date	Reps	Date
5-Repetition Back Squat Max test	3							
	3							
	1							
	1							
	5							
Hammer Back Machine	8							
	8							
	8							
Push/Pull Circuit	5							
Biceps Curl	10							
	10							
	10							
Body composition testing all week								
Split Squat	6							
	6							
Height and Weight test								

Wednesday	Reps	Date	Reps	Date	Reps	Date	Reps	Date
225 Reps (test)*								
Three-Way Raise (front, lateral, rear)	3 sets							
Tate Press	10							
	10							
	10							
5-Repetition Bench Max test*	3							
	3							
	2							
	1							
	1							
	1							
Hammer Back Machine	8							
	8							
	8							

(continued)

Table 10.13, *continued*

Friday								
	Reps	**Date**	**Reps**	**Date**	**Reps**	**Date**	**Reps**	**Date**
1-Repetition Speed Clean Max test	1							
	1							
	1							
	1							
	1							
	1							
Hip and Groin Flexibility test (V-Sit, Sit and Reach)								
Max Pull-Up test								
Four-Way Neck	2 × 10							
Ab Circuit	3 sets							
All retests completed								

M = maximum repetitions (as many reps as possible)
The 225 Reps and 5-Repetition Max tests should be done on different weeks.

Postlift Activity

1. Supplemental (see Supplemental Exercises)
2. Correctives (based on Gray Cook's functional movement screen)
3. Hip and shoulder mobility
4. Regeneration through static and partner stretching, foam rolling, hydrotherapy (see Recovery in chapter 3)

SUPPLEMENTAL EXERCISES

Supplemental exercises are performed after the central portion of the workout. These exercises are separated into stages, each with a specific purpose. Stage 1 exercises are corrective exercises designed to eliminate asymmetries, imbalances, and functional weaknesses, and are based on Gray Cook's functional movement screen as mentioned in chapter 2. Stage 2 (table 10.14) and stage 3 (table 10.15) exercises are further broken down into position categories to address the needs of the position as well as the athlete. Stage 2 supplemental exercises are strength-based exercises designed to target muscular weaknesses. Stage 3 supplemental exercises are skill-based exercises designed to transfer the athlete's abilities from the weight room to the fundamentals on the football field. The supplemental exercises can also be used to perform extra workouts if desired.

Table 10.14 Stage 2 Supplemental Exercises

	Strength		Power	
	Exercise	**Reps**	**Exercise**	**Reps**
OL, DL	Sledgehammer Hammer Back Machine Face Pull Push-Up Split Squat	1 × 10 2 × 10 2 × 20 2 × M 2 × 10	Box Jump Medicine Ball Chest Pass (staggered)	2 × 5 2 × 5
TE, RB, LB	Rice Bucket Hammer Back Machine Push-Up Walking Lunge	2 × 50 2 × 10 2 × M 2 × 10	Calf Shock Drop Balance Drill Medicine Ball Chest Pass (single leg)	2 × 8 2 × 5 2 × 5
DB, WR	Rice Bucket Hammer Back Machine Push-Up Reverse Walking Lunge	2 × 50 2 × 10 2 × M 2 × 10	Calf Shock Drop Altitude Drop Medicine Ball Chest Pass (with step)	2 × 8 2 × 5 2 × 5
QB, K, P	Wrist Roller Hammer Back Machine Hanging Knee Raise Rear Shoulder Raise (QB) Step-Up	2 × 10 2 × 10 2 × M 2 × 10 2 × 10	Calf Shock Drop Altitude Drop Overhead Throwdown	2 × 8 2 × 5 2 × 5

Table 10.15 Stage 3 Supplemental Exercises

	Strength		Power		Agility	
	Exercise	**Reps**	**Exercise**	**Reps**	**Exercise**	**Reps**
OL, DL	Tire Flip	2 × 5	Jammer Extension Squat Jump Plyometric Push-Up Slide Board (20 sec.)	2 × 5 2 × 5 2 × 5 2 sets	Speed Ladder Drill	1 drill × 3 reps
TE, RB, LB	Plate Push	3 × 25 yards	Jammer Extension Depth Jump Plyometric Push-Up Slide Board (20 sec.)	2 × 5 2 × 3 2 × 5 2 sets	Speed Ladder Drill	1 drill × 3 reps
DB, WR	Sled Pull	3 × 25 yards	Jammer Extension Depth Jump Plyometric Push-Up Slide Board (20 sec.)	2 × 5 2 × 3 2 × 5 2 sets	Speed Ladder Drill	1 drill × 3 reps
QB, K, P	Sled Pull	3 × 25 yards	Depth Jump Slide Board (20 sec.)	2 × 3 2 sets	Speed Ladder Drill	1 drill × 3 reps

CONCLUSION

There are many ways to design a workout program. Ultimately, the best program is the one that can be coached and performed consistently with passion and attention to detail. The one common denominator among all the best programs is that they are ever evolving and always being improved.

Chapter 11

Spring and Summer Workouts

S pring football workouts are very similar to in-season workouts (see chapter 12) in that playing football becomes the priority. Lifting weights and conditioning become secondary, although strength gains in the weight room can still be achieved with careful planning. Level one and level two players still need more strength development, and the workout can be designed to address this need. More developed players can dedicate less time to strength development and more time to explosive training and regeneration.

Summer football workouts are similar to off-season workouts (see chapter 10) in that making gains to improve athleticism and strength, not playing football, is the primary focus. As the football season approaches, you must focus on movement and prepare yourself to play football to the best of your abilities while reducing your chance of injury. If you are participating in seven-on-seven drills during the summer, this should be taken into consideration when evaluating your overall training volume.

SPRING WORKOUTS

During spring football, lifting consists of two total-body sessions per week. The first workout uses the Hang Clean and Squat as the core lifts. The second workout features the Bench Press as the core lift.

If you choose to do an extra workout for upper-body strength improvement, complete it on Friday afternoon before practice. Running conditioning is incorporated into the practice routine.

Spring Training Tempo in the Weight Room

During spring football, your training tempo is controlled mainly by super-setting all auxiliary exercises. No players are allowed to sit or stand around during the training session. For the majority of the team, because maintaining strength, stability, and mobility are the primary goals, maximal recovery between working sets is not a priority as it is in the off-season or summer.

Spring Training Programs

The spring training programs (tables 11.1 and 11.2) are designed to maintain the strength and power gained during the off-season program. The spring training program introduces more mobility, stability, and flexibility because you are now practicing and need more help recovering. If you need to get stronger, you can do so with strength-building exercises as your supplemental work (stage 2).

Prelift Activity

1. Dynamic warm-up
2. Stretch
3. Core
4. Rotator Cuff and Scap Circuit
5. Neck

Table 11.1 Spring Ball Levels One and Two

| | Monday | | | | | | | |
	Reps	Date	Reps	Date	Reps	Date	Reps	Date
Hang Clean	3							
	3							
	3							
	3							
Back Squat	3							
	3							
	3							
	3							
Standing Shoulder Press	8							
	8							
	8							
Hammer Back Machine	10							
	10							
	10							

Monday *(continued)*								
	Reps	**Date**	**Reps**	**Date**	**Reps**	**Date**	**Reps**	**Date**
Two-Way Raise (lateral, rear)	2 sets							
Reverse Hyperextension	10							
	10							
Wednesday								
	Reps	**Date**	**Reps**	**Date**	**Reps**	**Date**	**Reps**	**Date**
Hang Clean Complex (Power Shrug × 3, High Pull 2, Hang Clean 1)	3 sets							
Bench Press	5							
	4							
	3							
	M							
Triceps Extension	10							
	10							
Pistol Squat	10							
	10							
Pull-Up	M							
	M							
	M							
Romanian Dead Lift (RDL)	8							
	8							
Two-Way Raise (lateral, rear)	2 sets							
Glute Ham Raise	10							
	10							

M = maximum repetitions (as many reps as possible)

Table 11.2   Spring Ball Levels Three and Four

Monday								
	Reps	**Date**	**Reps**	**Date**	**Reps**	**Date**	**Reps**	**Date**
Hang Clean (Tendo at 1.55 m/s)	3							
	3							
	3							
	3							
Box Squat (Tendo at 0.8 m/s)	3							
	3							
	3							
	3							
Standing Shoulder Press	8							
	8							
	8							
Hammer Back Machine	10							
	10							
	10							
Reverse Hyperextension	10							
	10							
Wednesday								
	Reps	**Date**	**Reps**	**Date**	**Reps**	**Date**	**Reps**	**Date**
Box Jump (dumbbell)	5							
	5							
	5							
Board Bench Press	3							
	3							
	3							
	3							
Pistol Squat	10							
	10							
Pull-Up	M							
	M							
	M							
Romanian Dead Lift (RDL)	8							
	8							

M = maximum repetitions (as many reps as possible)

Postlift Activity
- Supplemental (see Supplemental Exercises in chapter 10)
- Correctives based on Gray Cook's functional movement screen
- Hip and shoulder mobility
- Regeneration through static and partner stretching, foam rolling, and hydrotherapy (see Recovery in chapter 3)

SUMMER WORKOUTS

The summer lifting routine consists of a four-day split (Monday, Tuesday, Thursday, and Friday) with Wednesday used as a recovery and regeneration day for activities such as yoga, pool time, and ice baths (table 11.3). The lifting format is similar to that of the off-season except that each day focuses on either the upper or lower body. Each day begins with the core lift followed by auxiliary and supplemental exercises.

Running precedes lifting during the summer to emphasize competitive movement training and conditioning consistently. Each day is formatted to train speed technique, acceleration, lateral speed and agility, plyometric acceleration, or anaerobic conditioning.

Multilevel Progression

Level zero training takes place during the first half of the summer, and level one training takes place during the second half of the summer, followed by testing. At this point, all level one athletes will be promoted either to Gun Club (see chapter 12) if they are red-shirted or to level two if they are on the travel squad.

Players who were at level zero and level one during the spring are promoted to level two (strength) for the start of the summer training program. Players who begin level zero during on-campus training in the summer move to level two or Gun Club in the fall. Promotions to levels three and four occur before the summer training begins.

Table 11.3 Order of Activities for Summer Training

Day of the week	Activities
Monday	1. Speed warm-up and flexibility 2. Bridge Series 3. Leg Swing 4. Speed station (A-Skip, B-Skip, C-Skip, Dead Leg, Fast Leg, Form Run) 5. Lift (see workout cards)
Tuesday	1. Agility warm-up and flexibility 2. Balance Drills 3. Agility station (Five-Cone, Six-Bag, RACE, Ladder Drill) 4. Lift (see workout cards)
Wednesday	Active rest (yoga, hydrotherapy, massage therapy)
Thursday	1. Agility warm-up and flexibility 2. Bridge Series 3. Balance Drills 4. Anaerobic power development (Play Drives, 106s, 300-Yard Shuttle, 110s, PTs, Full Gassers) 5. Lift (see workout cards)
Friday	1. All-fours warm-up and flexibility 2. Bridge Series 3. Leg Swings 4. Plyometric drills 5. Acceleration drills (Stadium Stairs, Build-Up, Uphill Run, Downhill Run, Partner Resistance, Scramble-Ups) 6. Lift (see workout cards)

Summer Training Tempo in the Weight Room

The summer training tempo allows for total or near total recovery between the core lifts and auxiliary strength-based exercises. As the training cycle gets closer to the testing period, you are allowed to sit between sets to speed up recovery. This tempo allows for maximal strength gains. Once you have completed all strength- and power-based exercises, you should increase your training tempo through the completion of your workout.

Summer Training Programs

The summer training programs build on the strength and power gained during the off-season and capitalize on the mobility, flexibility, and stability work done during the spring. The summer training programs (tables 11.4 through 11.12) focus more on conditioning, plyometrics, agility, lateral speed, and acceleration. This is the most critical training period because the training must prepare you for the rigors of preseason camp and the competition season.

Prelift Activity

1. Dynamic warm-up
2. Stretch
3. Core
4. Rotator Cuff and Scap Circuit
5. Neck

Postlift Activity

- Supplemental (see Supplemental Exercises in chapter 10)
- Correctives based on Gray Cook's functional movement screen
- Hip and shoulder mobility
- Regeneration through static and partner stretching, foam rolling, and hydrotherapy (see Recovery in chapter 3)

Table 11.4 Summer Workout Level Zero

Workout 1								
Body weight circuit	**Reps**	**Date**	**Reps**	**Date**	**Reps**	**Date**	**Reps**	**Date**
Body Weight Squat	2 × 20							
Push-Up	2 × 20							
Split Squat	2 × 20							
Team circuit*	**Reps**	**Date**	**Reps**	**Date**	**Reps**	**Date**	**Reps**	**Date**
Medicine Ball Chest Pass								
Plate Push								
Overhead Stair Walk								
Walking Lunge								
Ab exercise of choice								
Workout 2								
Body weight circuit	**Reps**	**Date**	**Reps**	**Date**	**Reps**	**Date**	**Reps**	**Date**
Split Jump	2 × 20							
Plate Push	6 × 15 yards							
Pull-Ups	20 total reps							
Team circuit*	**Reps**	**Date**	**Reps**	**Date**	**Reps**	**Date**	**Reps**	**Date**
Front Bear Crawl								
Push-Up								

(continued)

Table 11.4, *continued*

Workout 2 *(continued)*								
Team circuit*	**Reps**	**Date**	**Reps**	**Date**	**Reps**	**Date**	**Reps**	**Date**
Walking Lunge								
Squat Jump								
Ab exercise of choice								
Workout 3								
Body weight circuit	**Reps**	**Date**	**Reps**	**Date**	**Reps**	**Date**	**Reps**	**Date**
Push-Up	2 × 20							
Body Weight Squat	2 × 20							
Inverted Row	2 × 20							
Team circuit*	**Reps**	**Date**	**Reps**	**Date**	**Reps**	**Date**	**Reps**	**Date**
Spiderman								
Walking Lunge								
Lateral Walking Lunge								
Jump Squat								
Ab exercise of choice								

*Perform team circuits as a team with set parameters for successful completion together. The coach decides the repetitions before the start of the exercise. Everyone counts the repetitions. Effort levels for all must be high with no one missing a repetition.

Table 11.5 Summer Workout Level One

Monday								
	Reps	**Date**	**Reps**	**Date**	**Reps**	**Date**	**Reps**	**Date**
Bench Press	10							
APRE6	6							
	M							
	M							
Triceps Extension	10							
	10							
	10							
Biceps Curl	10							
	10							
	10							
Ab Circuit	2 sets							
Six-Way Neck With Manual Resistance	10							
Tuesday								
	Reps	**Date**	**Reps**	**Date**	**Reps**	**Date**	**Reps**	**Date**
Hang Clean Complex (Power Shrug × 3, High Pull × 2, Hang Clean × 1)	3 sets							

Tuesday *(continued)*	Reps	Date	Reps	Date	Reps	Date	Reps	Date
Hang Clean	5							
	5							
	5							
Hammer Back Machine	8							
	8							
	8							
Romanian Dead Lift (RDL)	10							
	10							
	10							
Pistol Squat	8							
	8							
	8							

Thursday	Reps	Date	Reps	Date	Reps	Date	Reps	Date
225 Reps (test)	M							
Romanian Dead Lift (RDL)	10							
	10							
	10							
Hammer Back Machine	8							
	8							
	8							
Triceps Extension	10							
	10							
	10							
Six-Way Neck With Manual Resistance	10							

Friday	Reps	Date	Reps	Date	Reps	Date	Reps	Date
Back Squat	10							
APRE6	6							
	M							
	M							
Max Pull-Up test	M							
Barbell Row	10							
	10							
	10							
Pistol Squat	8							
	8							
	8							
Four-Way Neck	10							

M = maximum repetitions (as many reps as possible)

Table 11.6   Summer Workout Level Two, Phase One

Monday								
	Reps	**Date**	**Reps**	**Date**	**Reps**	**Date**	**Reps**	**Date**
Bench Press	10							
APRE6	6							
	M							
	M							
Triceps Extension (barbell)	15							
	15							
	15							
Inverted Row (barbell)	6							
	6							
	6							
Shoulder Combo 6-8-8-10	2 sets							
Reverse Hyperextension	10							
Max Pull-Up Test	M							
Tuesday								
	Reps	**Date**	**Reps**	**Date**	**Reps**	**Date**	**Reps**	**Date**
Hang Clean	6							
APRE3	3							
	M							
	M							
Front Squat	8							
	8							
	8							
One-Arm Dumbbell Row	8							
	8							
	8							
Pistol Squat	8							
	8							
	8							
Good Morning	20							
	20							
	20							
Biceps Curl (barbell)	12							
	12							
	12							

Thursday								
	Reps	**Date**	**Reps**	**Date**	**Reps**	**Date**	**Reps**	**Date**
Power Shrug	6							
	6							
	6							
Incline Bench Press	10							
	10							
	10							
Standing Shoulder Press	8							
	8							
	8							
Barbell Row	8							
	8							
	8							
Band Pull-Apart (mini band)	20							
	20							
Triceps Pushdown	20							
(light band)	20							
Three-Way Raise (rear, lateral, front)	2 sets							
Friday								
	Reps	**Date**	**Reps**	**Date**	**Reps**	**Date**	**Reps**	**Date**
Back Squat	10							
APRE6	6							
	M							
	M							
Pull-Up	10							
	10							
	10							
Romanian Dead Lift (RDL)	10							
	10							
	10							
Band X-Walk (light band)	10							
	10							
	10							
Hammer Back Machine	12							

(continued)

Table 11.6, *continued*

	Friday *(continued)*							
	Reps	**Date**	**Reps**	**Date**	**Reps**	**Date**	**Reps**	**Date**
	12							
	12							
Glute Ham Raise	8							
	8							
	8							

M = maximum repetitions (as many reps as possible)

Table 11.7   Summer Workout Level Two, Phase One

	Monday							
	Reps	**Date**	**Reps**	**Date**	**Reps**	**Date**	**Reps**	**Date**
Bench Press	6							
APRE3	3							
	M							
	M							
Triceps Extension (barbell)	15							
	15							
	15							
Inverted Row (barbell)	6							
	6							
	6							
Shoulder Combo 6-8-8-10	2 sets							
Reverse Hyperextension	10							
Max Pull-Up Test	M							
	Tuesday							
	Reps	**Date**	**Reps**	**Date**	**Reps**	**Date**	**Reps**	**Date**
Hang Clean	6							
APRE3	3							
	M							
	M							
Front Squat	8							
	8							
	8							
One-Arm Dumbbell Row	8							
	8							
	8							

Tuesday *(continued)*								
	Reps	**Date**	**Reps**	**Date**	**Reps**	**Date**	**Reps**	**Date**
Pistol Squat	8							
	8							
	8							
Good Morning	20							
	20							
	20							
Biceps Curl (barbell)	12							
	12							
	12							
Thursday								
	Reps	**Date**	**Reps**	**Date**	**Reps**	**Date**	**Reps**	**Date**
Power Shrug	6							
	6							
	6							
Incline Bench Press	8							
	8							
	8							
Standing Shoulder Press	6							
	6							
	6							
Barbell Row	8							
	8							
	8							
Band Pull-Apart (mini band)	20							
	20							
Triceps Pushdown (light band)	20							
	20							
Three-Way Raise (rear, lateral, front)	2 sets							
Friday								
	Reps	**Date**	**Reps**	**Date**	**Reps**	**Date**	**Reps**	**Date**
Back Squat	6							
APRE3	3							
	M							
	M							

(continued)

Table 11.7, *continued*

Friday *(continued)*								
	Reps	**Date**	**Reps**	**Date**	**Reps**	**Date**	**Reps**	**Date**
Pull-Up	10							
	10							
	10							
Romanian Dead Lift (RDL)	8							
	8							
	8							
Band X-Walk (light band)	10							
	10							
	10							
Hammer Back Machine	8							
	8							
	8							
Glute Ham Raise	8							
	8							
	8							

M = maximum repetitions (as many reps as possible)

Table 11.8   Summer Workout Level Three, Phase One

Monday								
	Reps	**Date**	**Reps**	**Date**	**Reps**	**Date**	**Reps**	**Date**
Bench Press (close grip)	10							
APRE6	6							
	M							
	M							
Dumbbell Incline Bench Press	8							
	8							
	8							
Triceps Extension	8							
	8							
	8							
Barbell Row	8							
	8							
	8							
Shoulder Combo 6-8-8-10	2 sets							
Inverted Row (pause 3 sec. at chest)	6							
	6							

Tuesday								
	Reps	**Date**	**Reps**	**Date**	**Reps**	**Date**	**Reps**	**Date**
Hang Clean (Tendo at 1.55 m/s)	3							
	3							
	3							
	3							
Box Squat (Tendo at 0.8 m/s)	2							
	2							
	2							
	2							
	2							
Pistol Squat	8							
	8							
	8							
Glute Ham Raise	8							
	8							
	8							
Biceps Curl	8							
	8							
	8							
Thursday								
	Reps	**Date**	**Reps**	**Date**	**Reps**	**Date**	**Reps**	**Date**
Bench Press (Tendo at 0.8 m/s)	3							
	3							
	3							
	3							
	3							
	3							
Board Bench Press	3							
	3							
	3							
Tate Press	M							
	M							
Pull-Up	M							
	M							
	M							
Three-Way Raise	2 sets							
Low Row	10							
	10							

(continued)

Table 11.8, *continued*

	Friday							
	Reps	**Date**	**Reps**	**Date**	**Reps**	**Date**	**Reps**	**Date**
Back Squat	5							
	5							
	5							
	5							
	5							
Walking Lunge (dumbbells)	6							
	6							
	6							
Reverse Hyperextension	8							
	8							
	8							
Leg Curl	10							
	10							
Band Pull-Apart (mini band)	15							
	15							
Biceps Curl	10							
	10							
	10							

M = maximum repetitions (as many reps as possible)

Table 11.9 Summer Workout Level Three, Phase Two

	Monday							
	Reps	**Date**	**Reps**	**Date**	**Reps**	**Date**	**Reps**	**Date**
Bench Press	6							
APRE3	3							
	M							
	M							
Horizontal Cable Press	8							
	8							
	8							
Tate Press	M							
	M							
One-Arm Dumbbell Row	8							
	8							
	8							
Shoulder Circuit with dumbbells 6-6-6-6-6	2 sets							

Monday *(continued)*								
	Reps	**Date**	**Reps**	**Date**	**Reps**	**Date**	**Reps**	**Date**
Inverted Row (suspended)	6							
	6							
Tuesday								
	Reps	**Date**	**Reps**	**Date**	**Reps**	**Date**	**Reps**	**Date**
Hang Clean (Tendo at 1.55 m/s)	3							
	3							
	3							
	3							
Box Squat (Tendo at 0.8 m/s)	2							
	2							
	2							
	2							
	2							
Split Squat (barbell)	6							
	6							
	6							
Glute Ham Raise	8							
	8							
	8							
Biceps Curl	8							
	8							
	8							
Thursday								
	Reps	**Date**	**Reps**	**Date**	**Reps**	**Date**	**Reps**	**Date**
Bench Press (Tendo at 0.8 m/s)	3							
	3							
	3							
	3							
	3							
	3							
225 Reps (test)	M							
Triceps Extension (dumbbell)	8							
	8							
	8							

(continued)

Table 11.9, *continued*

Thursday *(continued)*								
	Reps	**Date**	**Reps**	**Date**	**Reps**	**Date**	**Reps**	**Date**
Pull-Up	M							
	M							
	M							
Cuban Press (dumbbell, incline)	10							
	10							
Hammer Back Machine (4 sec. eccentric)	8							
	8							
Friday								
	Reps	**Date**	**Reps**	**Date**	**Reps**	**Date**	**Reps**	**Date**
Back Squat	3							
	3							
	3							
	3							
	3							
Walking Lunge (dumbbells)	6							
	6							
	6							
Reverse Hyperextension	8							
	8							
	8							
Leg Curl	10							
	10							
Face Pull	15							
	15							
Biceps Curl	8							
	8							
	8							

M = maximum repetitions (as many reps as possible)

Table 11.10　Summer Workout Level Four, Phase One

Monday								
	Reps	**Date**	**Reps**	**Date**	**Reps**	**Date**	**Reps**	**Date**
Floor Press (barbell)	3							
	3							
	3							
	3							
	3							
	3							
Horizontal Cable Press	8							
	8							
	8							
Triceps Pushdown (light band)	M							
One-Arm Dumbbell Row	6							
	6							
	6							
Shoulder Combo 6-8-8-10	2 sets							
Inverted Row (pause 3 sec. at chest)	6							
	6							
Tuesday								
	Reps	**Date**	**Reps**	**Date**	**Reps**	**Date**	**Reps**	**Date**
Hang Clean (Tendo at 1.55 m/s)	2							
	2							
	2							
	2							
	2							
	2							
Box Squat (Tendo at 0.8 m/s)	2							
	2							
	2							
	2							
	2							
Split Squat (barbell)	6							
	6							
Reverse Hyperextension	8							
	8							
	8							

(continued)

Table 11.10, *continued*

Thursday								
	Reps	**Date**	**Reps**	**Date**	**Reps**	**Date**	**Reps**	**Date**
Bench Press (Tendo at 0.8 m/s)	3							
	3							
	3							
	3							
	3							
	3							
Push-Up (30 sec. each set)	3 sets							
Pull-Up	M							
	M							
	M							
Triceps Extension (dumbbells)	8							
	8							
	8							
Three-Way Raise	2 sets							
Face Pull	20							
	20							
Friday								
	Reps	**Date**	**Reps**	**Date**	**Reps**	**Date**	**Reps**	**Date**
Dead Lift	5							
	4							
	3							
	2							
	1							
Step-Up	6							
	6							
	6							
Glute Ham Raise	8							
	8							
	8							

M = maximum repetitions (as many reps as possible)

Table 11.11 Summer Workout Level Four, Phase Two

Monday	Reps	Date	Reps	Date	Reps	Date	Reps	Date
Board Bench Press (barbell)	3							
	3							
	3							
	3							
	3							
	3							
Horizontal Cable Press	8							
	8							
	8							
Triceps Pushdown (average band)	M							
One-Arm Dumbbell Row	6							
	6							
	6							
Inverted Row (pause 4 sec. at chest)	6							
	6							
Tuesday	Reps	Date	Reps	Date	Reps	Date	Reps	Date
Hang Clean (Tendo at 1.55 m/s)	2							
	2							
	2							
	2							
	2							
	2							
Box Squat (Tendo at 0.8 m/s with chains)	2							
	2							
	2							
	2							
	2							
Split Squat (barbell)	6							
	6							

(continued)

Table 11.11, *continued*

Tuesday *(continued)*								
	Reps	**Date**	**Reps**	**Date**	**Reps**	**Date**	**Reps**	**Date**
Reverse Hyperextension	8							
	8							
	8							
Thursday								
	Reps	**Date**	**Reps**	**Date**	**Reps**	**Date**	**Reps**	**Date**
Bench Press (Tendo at 0.8 m/s with mini bands)	3							
	3							
	3							
	3							
	3							
	3							
Push-Up (30 sec. each set)	3 sets							
Hammer Back Machine	8							
	8							
	8							
Triceps Extension (dumbbells)	8							
	8							
	8							
Three-Way Raise	2 sets							
Cuban Press	10							
	10							
Friday								
	Reps	**Date**	**Reps**	**Date**	**Reps**	**Date**	**Reps**	**Date**
Back Squat	5							
	4							
	3							
	2							
	1							
Step-Up	6							
	6							
	6							
Glute Ham Raise (with iso hold)	6							
	6							
	6							

M = maximum repetitions (as many reps as possible)

Table 11.12 Summer Workout Level Four, Phase Three

Monday	Reps	Date	Reps	Date	Reps	Date	Reps	Date
Bench Press	5							
	4							
	3							
	2							
	1							
	1							
Dumbbell Incline Bench Press	6							
	6							
	6							
Triceps Pushdown (average band)	1 set							
Barbell Row	6							
	6							
	6							
Shoulder Circuit with dumbbells 6-6-6-6-6-6	2 sets							
Inverted Row (pause 5 sec. at chest)	6							
	6							

Tuesday	Reps	Date	Reps	Date	Reps	Date	Reps	Date
Hang Clean (Tendo at 0.8 m/s)	1							
	1							
	1							
	1							
	1							
	1							
Box Squat (Tendo at 0.8 m/s with bands)	2							
	2							
	2							
	2							
	2							
Reverse Hyperextension	8							
	8							
	8							

(continued)

Table 11.12, *continued*

Thursday								
	Reps	Date	Reps	Date	Reps	Date	Reps	Date
Bench Press (Tendo at 0.8 m/s with chains)	3							
	3							
	3							
	3							
	3							
	3							
225 Bench Rep Test	M							
Hammer Back Machine	10							
	8							
	6							
Triceps Extension (dumbbells)	8							
	8							
	8							
Three-Way Raise	2 sets							
Face Pull	20							
	20							
Friday								
	Reps	Date	Reps	Date	Reps	Date	Reps	Date
Walking Lunge (barbell)	6							
	6							
	6							
Slide Board	2 × 20 sec.							
Glute Ham Raise	10							
	10							
	10							

M = maximum repetitions (as many reps as possible)

CONCLUSION

When designing a training program, remember to take all training aspects into consideration. Make sure the demands placed on athletes are evaluated and considered every year by the coach. Each phase of programming should build on the foundation and prepare you for the next phase. Your entire career should be taken into consideration at each phase.

Chapter 12

In-Season Workouts

Because of the physical nature of preseason training camp, also known as two-a-days, weight training must be highly focused on recovery and regeneration. Prioritizing recovery and regeneration will allow you to maintain range of motion and mobility. Maintaining stability in the joints will help reduce the risk of injury. Focusing on recovery and regeneration exercises allows for better strength maintenance. Use exercises designed to promote blood circulation to eliminate waste rather than those designed to develop strength.

Maintaining strength, mobility, and stability is the primary focus of in-season training. Most football workout training programs should not focus on increasing strength during the season. Football practice and games should be the focal point. Using a flush workout (also known as recovery) following the day of a game or intense practice can be useful when used in conjunction with the weight training session. For example, if a one-hour workout is scheduled, spend 30 minutes on flushing and 30 minutes on weight training. Incorporating recovery allows the muscles to do their job of absorbing and producing force.

Players who join the team at the beginning of training camp or the first day of classes are in Gun Club, which is considered level one, if they are red-shirting. If they are not red-shirting and are on the travel squad, they are assigned to level two, which is the progressive resistance training program.

PRESEASON TRAINING

Preseason lifting consists of a 25- to 30-minute, total-body training routine. Workouts can be rotated by position groups according to the practice schedule during camp. Conditioning can be incorporated into the practice routine.

Preseason Training Tempo in the Weight Room

During the preseason or training camp, training is fast paced to keep the energy level up and to maximize the efficiency of training time, especially because football players are already exhausted. These workouts are very short and promote recovery through blood circulation and regeneration techniques. No players are allowed to walk or stand still at any time during the workout.

Preseason Training Programs

The training program for the preseason (table 12.1) alternates two short total-body training sessions throughout camp. As already mentioned, because recovery is important during this time, the lower-body exercise volume and intensity are reduced. The focus of workouts in the preseason should be on mobility and efficiency. Each workout should be no longer than 30 minutes from start to finish.

Prelift Activity

1. Dynamic warm-up

Table 12.1   Preseason Workouts

Workout 1					
	Goal	**Weight**	**Reps**	**Weight**	**Reps**
Six-Way Neck With Manual Resistance (team)	1 × 10				
Scap Circuit	1 set				
Rotator Cuff Circuit	1 set				
Push-Up	3 × 25				
Reverse Hyperextension or Romanian Dead Lift (RDL) (dumbbell)	2 × 8				
One-Arm Dumbbell Row	3 × 8				
Crunch	1 × 50				
Recovery (foam roll, static stretch)	As needed				
Workout 2					
	Goal	**Weight**	**Reps**	**Weight**	**Reps**
Six-Way Neck With Manual Resistance (team)	1 × 10				
Push/Pull Circuit	5 reps each				
Bench Press (dumbbell)	3 × 6				
Cuban Press	2 × 15				
Pistol Squat	2 × 8				
Hammer Back Machine	3 × 8				
Oblique Crunch	25 each side				
Recovery (foam roll, static stretch)	As needed				

Postlift Activity

1. Hip and shoulder mobility
2. Recovery through static and partner stretching, foam rolling, and hydrotherapy (see chapter 3)

IN-SEASON TRAINING FOR A TRAVEL SQUAD

Travel squad players lift twice a week, on Sunday and Wednesday. The first workout features the Squat as the core lift. This workout is preceded by a flush (an extended warm-up) to increase blood flow in the body and give more time for tendons and ligaments to warm up. The increased blood flow helps the body discard blood from damaged tissue and prepare for the workout.

The second in-season workout for the travel squad features the Hang Clean and Bench Press as the core lifts. Some football players are designated for a third lift day (Friday), in which they perform a workout targeting improvements in upper-body strength and mobility.

Players are further separated into a progressive resistance group and an autoregulatory group. The progressive resistance (level two) players are those who need improvement in overall strength and will benefit from percentage-based training. The autoregulatory (levels three and four) group is trained on the Hang Clean and Squat using the Tendo unit. The Tendo allows these lifters to adjust the weight to meet the speed requirements as dictated by the status of the central nervous system. For instance, following a game that was taxing on the central nervous system, higher speeds and lesser weights are designated for the entire week.

Running and conditioning are incorporated at the end of practice. Some examples of conditioning drills used are 106s and PTs (see chapter 9).

In-Season Training Tempo in the Weight Room

During the season, training tempo is controlled mainly by supersetting all auxiliary exercises. No players are allowed to sit or stand around during the training session. For the majority of the team, maintaining strength, stability, and mobility is the primary goal. Maximal recovery between working sets is not a priority as it is during the off-season or summer.

In-Season Training Programs

In-season training (tables 12.2 and 12.3) is the longest training period during the year. Level-two players have the opportunity to make strength gains during this time, and the program is designed as such. The level-three and level-four workouts are designed according to the schedule and factors such as the day and time of the game and whether it is home or away. For example, after a late game on the road you would incorporate light training Tendo speeds for the following week of training. The focus of in-season is to be as powerful as possible and to demonstrate your preparation to deliver your best.

Prelift Activity

1. Flush. This portion of the workout is essentially an extended warm-up to increase blood flow and provide more time for tendons and ligaments to warm up. The increased blood flow helps damaged tissue and prepares the body for the workout.

Table 12.2 In-Season Gun Club Level 1 Workouts

Monday							
	Reps	**Date**	**Reps**	**Date**	**Reps**	**Date**	**Reps**
Back Squat APRE6	10 6 M M						
Bench Press (strip set)	1 set						
One-Arm Dumbbell Row (work the rack)	1 set						
Farmer's Walk	3 × 30 yd.						
Triceps Pushdown (work the stack)	1 set						
Wednesday							
	Reps	**Date**	**Reps**	**Date**	**Reps**	**Date**	**Reps**
Bench Press APRE6	10 6 M M						
Walking Lunge (Gun Club exercise 1)	2 × 10 each leg						
Pull-Up (Gun Club exercise 2)	3 × M						
Tire Flips (Gun Club exercise 3)	2 × 20 yd.						
Biceps Curl (work the stack; Gun Club exercise 4)	1 set						
Friday							
	Reps	**Date**	**Reps**	**Date**	**Reps**	**Date**	**Reps**
Hang Clean Complex (Power Shrug × 3, High Pull × 2, Hang Clean × 1)	3 sets						
Romanian Dead Lift (barbell; Gun Club exercise 1)	3 × 10						
Push-Up (Gun Club exercise 2)	3 × M						
Prowler Push (Gun Club exercise 3)	4 × 20 yd.						
Band Pushdown (light band; Gun Club exercise 4)	1 min.						

M = maximum repetitions (as many reps as possible)

Table 12.3 In-Season Workouts: Levels Two, Three, and Four

Lift 1							
Flush Workout: Dynamic warm-up Bridge Series Four-Way Neck (isometric) Leg Swing Romanian Dead Lift (RDL) Reverse Walking Lunge Rotator Cuff Extended Squat Hurdle Series	 1 set 1 set 1 × 10 2 × 6 2 × 6 1 set 1 × 10 1 set						
	Goal	**Weight**	**Reps**	**Weight**	**Reps**	**Weight**	**Reps**
Back Squat Levels three and four Tendo at 0.6 to 1.0 m/s	3 3 3 3						
Bench Press (dumbbell), Incline Bench Press (dumbbell), or Horizontal Cable Press	8 8 8						
High Lat Pulldown, Low Row, or One-Arm Dumbbell Row	8 8 8						
Two-Way Raise (lateral and rear)	2 sets						
Lift 2							
Dynamic warm-up Bridge Series Scap Circuit Six-Way Neck With Manual Resistance (eccentric and concentric) Ab exercise of choice Hurdle Series							
	Goal	**Weight**	**Reps**	**Weight**	**Reps**	**Weight**	**Reps**
Hang Clean Levels three and four Tendo at 1.4 to 1.7 m/s	3 3 3						
Bench Press (barbell, variations)	3 to 5 3 to 5 3 to 5 3 to 5						
Walking Lunge, Reverse Walking Lunge, or Lateral Walking Lunge	8 8 8						

(continued)

Table 12.3, *continued*

Lift 2 *(continued)*						
	Goal	**Weight**	**Reps**	**Weight**	**Reps**	**Weight**	**Reps**
Hammer Back Machine	8 8 8						
Reverse Hyperextension	10 10						
Hamstring exercise: Leg Curl or Glute Ham Raise	8 8						

For level two, the Back Squat, Hang Clean, and Bench Press are regulated by progressive resistance. For levels three and four, the Back Squat and Hang Clean are regulated by Tendo speed, and the Bench Press is done to maximum effort.

Postlift Activity

1. Correctives based on Gray Cook's functional movement screen

2. Hip and shoulder mobility

3. Recovery through static and partner stretching, foam rolling, and hydrotherapy (chapter 3)

IN-SEASON TRAINING FOR RED-SHIRT PLAYERS

The Gun Club routine for red-shirt and nontravel players involves three total-body strength training sessions per week (Sunday, Wednesday, and Friday). Each session begins with a dynamic warm-up and stretch routine followed by core stabilization exercises. The first portion of the lifting workout begins with the core lift of the day—the Bench Press, Back Squat, or Hang Clean. Once the core lift is completed, the auxiliary and supplemental exercises follow. Supplemental exercises are used to address the particular weaknesses and needs of each player. The final portion of the workout consists of hip mobility and cool-down stretches.

Exercises in Gun Club are chosen based on these criteria:

- They challenge the mental capacity of each athlete.
- They increase motivation and competitiveness.
- They provide opportunities to work on the mirror muscles (guns) as well as the posterior chain.
- They use the repetition method exclusively (exercises to failure).
- They use unconventional exercises to provide variety.

Conditioning is incorporated into the practice routine or included as a part of weight training if the coach deems it necessary.

POSTSEASON TRAINING

If the team is bowl or playoff eligible, the postseason lifting phase can last three to four weeks depending on the date of the last regular season game and the date of the bowl game or the playoff schedule. The length of the championship season will determine the plan you follow during this phase. The general goals are to assist with the rehabilitation of injuries; improve the technical aspects of core lifts; and regain any losses in mobility, stability, or strength. This is a good time to address asymmetries, imbalances, and compensatory motor patterns. In other words, fix what has been broken. If the scenario is weekly playoff games, then staying with a training program similar to the in-season training program might be more beneficial. Conditioning is incorporated into the practice routine.

If the team is not bowl or playoff eligible, the goal of the postseason lifting phase is for maintaining a general level of fitness while giving the players time to recover physiologically and psychologically. Training at this time will differ from that used at other times of the year. The reps are typically in the 8 to 10 range. This stage can last from three to seven weeks depending on the date of the last game and when the off-season training program starts. The general goals are to rehabilitate injuries, improve the technical aspects of core lifts, and give you more autonomy in exercise selection. Running consists of general conditioning activities (aerobic and anaerobic) as well as athletic conditioning activities in other sports such as basketball and racquetball performed two or three times a week.

Postseason Training Tempo in the Weight Room

The postseason training tempo is controlled mainly by supersetting all exercises. No players are allowed to sit or stand around during the training session. For the majority of the team, maintaining strength, stability, and mobility is the primary goal. Maximal recovery between working sets is not a priority as it is during the off-season or summer.

Postseason Training Programs

Postseason training (tables 12.4 and 12.5) focuses on basic development exercises such as the Back Squat, Hang Clean, and Bench Press. At this point, regardless of whether you are eligible for postseason play, all levels have similar training programs. If you are going on to postseason play, you can treat the workouts as extended in-season training because the focus will still be on football. If you are not participating in postseason play, then it will essentially be a mini off-season with a shift back to building for the next competitive season.

Prelift Activity

1. Dynamic warm-up
2. Stretch
3. Core
4. Rotator Cuff and Scap Circuit
5. Neck

Table 12.4 Postseason Workouts With Bowl or Playoff: Levels One, Two, Three, and Four

Workout 1					
	Goal	**Weight**	**Reps**	**Weight**	**Reps**
Hang Clean (levels three and four, Tendo at 1.55 m/s)	6 × 3				
Bench Press (levels three and four, Tendo at 0.8 m/s)	6 × 3				
Back Squat (levels three and four, Tendo at 0.8 m/s)	6 × 2				
Hammer Back Machine	4 × 10				
Four-Way Neck	1 × 10				
Recovery (foam roll, static stretch)	As needed				
Workout 2					
	Goal	**Weight**	**Reps**	**Weight**	**Reps**
Bench Press (dumbbell, on physioball)	3 × 8				
Pistol Squat supersetted with Band X-Walk	3 × 8 3 × 8				
One-Arm Dumbbell Row supersetted with Four-Way Neck (superset first set only)	3 × 6 1 × 10				
Band Pull-Apart supersetted with Oblique Crunch	2 × 20 2 × 20				
Recovery (foam roll, static stretch)	As needed				

For levels one and two, the Back Squat, Hang Clean, and Bench Press are regulated by progressive resistance. For levels three and four, the Back Squat and Hang Clean are regulated by Tendo speed, and the Bench Press is done to maximum effort.

Table 12.5 Postseason Workouts With No Bowl or Playoff Game

Monday							
	Reps	Date	Reps	Date	Reps	Date	Reps
Back Squat (barbell)	10 10 10 10						
Standing Shoulder Press	10 10 10						
Barbell Row	10 10 10						
Push/Pull Circuit	5 5 5						
Pistol Squat	10 10 10						
Glute Ham Raise	8 8 8						
Wednesday							
	Reps	Date	Reps	Date	Reps	Date	Reps
Hang Clean	6 6 6 6						
Romanian Dead Lift (RDL) (barbell)	10 10 10						
Triceps Pushdown	1 min.						
Shoulder Combo 6-8-8-10	2 sets						
One-Arm Dumbbell Row	10 10 10						
Ab Circuit	3 sets						

(continued)

Table 12.5, *continued*

	Friday						
	Reps	**Date**	**Reps**	**Date**	**Reps**	**Date**	**Reps**
Bench Press (barbell)	10 10 10 10						
Front Squat	10 10 10						
Pull-Up (chin, neutral)	M M M						
Two-Way Raise (lateral, rear)	2 sets						
Ab Circuit	3 sets						
Lateral Walking Lunge	10 10						

M = maximum repetitions (as many reps as possible)

Postlift Activity

1. Hip and shoulder mobility
2. Recovery through static and partner stretching, foam rolling, and hydrotherapy (chapter 3)

CONCLUSION

Well-designed preseason, in-season, and postseason training programs can add to the potential of a football program. A poorly designed training program will detract from the potential of a football program. The ultimate goal of each phase of programming is to reduce the risk of injury, increase performance, and help keep the players on the field.

Additional Resources

INFORMATION ON SUPPLEMENTS

Drug-Free Sport: www.drugfreesport.com

International Society of Sports Nutrition: www.sportsnutritionsociety.org

National Collegiate Athletic Association: www.ncaa.org/health-safety

WEBSITES

Gray Cook's functional movement screen: www.functionalmovement.com

Louie Simmons of Westside Barbell: www.westside-barbell.com

JOURNAL ARTICLES AND BOOKS

Allaire, J.T. 2002. *The University of Tulsa Golden Hurricane Summer Conditioning Manual.*

Baroga, T.A.L. 1988. *Weightlifting: Fitness for All Sports.* Budapest, Hungary: International Weightlifting Federation.

Bompa, T.O and G.G. Haff. 2009. *Periodization: Theory and Methodology of Training.* Champaign, IL: Human Kinetics.

Bompa, T.O. 1996. *Periodization of Strength.* Toronto, ON: Veritas Publishing.

Fish, D.E., B.J. Krabak, D. Johnson-Green, B.J. DeLateur. 2003. Optimal resistance training: Comparison of DeLorme with Oxford techniques. American Journal of Physical Medicine and Rehabilitation 82(12): 903-909.

Fish, J. 2003. *The University of Missouri Summer Conditioning Manual.*

Kenn, J. 2003. *The Coaches Strength Training Playbook.* Monterey, CA, Coaches Choice.

Knight, K.L. 1985. Quadriceps strengthening with the DAPRE technique: Case studies with neurological implications. *Medicine and Science in Sports and Exercise.* 17(6): 646-50.

Mann, J.B., J.P. Thyfault, P.A. Ivey, and S.P. Sayers. 2010. The effects of auto-regulatory progressive resistance exercise vs. linear periodization on strength improvement in college athletes. *The Journal of Strength and Conditioning Research.* 24(7): 1718-1723.

National Strength and Conditioning Association. 2008. *Essentials of Strength Training and Conditioning, Third Edition.* Edited by T.R. Baechle and R.W. Earle. Champaign, IL: Human Kinetics.

Siff, M.C. 2000. *Supertraining.* Denver, CO.

Zatsiorsky, V.M. and W. Kraemer. 2006. *Science and Practice of Strength Training, Second Edition.* Champaign, IL, Human Kinetics.

Index

Note: Page references followed by an italic *f* or *t* indicate information contained in figures and tables, respectively.

A

agility development
　about 89-90
　agility station 95-98, 96*f*
　drills 91-102
　football agility training 90
　in-season 98
　mat drills station 92-95, 93*f*, 95*f*
　speed station 91
　summer ball 98
　testing 102
agility drills
　Combination Agilities 97-98
　Cone drills 97
　Five-Cone drills 100, 101*f*, 102*t*
　RACE drills 99*f*-100*f*
　Six-Bag drills 96*f*
　Speed Ladder drills 97
anthropomorphic measures 24-25
arousal levels 8
athletic position 103*f*
autoregulatory progressive resistance exercise (APRE) 191-192, 191*t*, 192*t*

B

back development
　Barbell Row 158-159, 158*f*
　Hammer Back Machine 160
　High Lat Pulldown 155
　Inverted Row 159*f*
　Iso High Row 160
　Iso Lateral DY (Dorian Yates) Row 160
　Iso Lateral Front Lat Pulldown 160
　Iso Lateral Low Row 161
　Iso Row 161
　Low Row 156-157, 157*f*
　One-Arm Dumbbell Row 156
　Pull-Up 158
balance 89
basic movement skills 10
biceps development
　Biceps Curl 173
　Weight Stack Curl 173
bodybuilding 134-135

C

carbohydrate 42, 45-46, 47
chest development
　Close Grip Bench Press 168
　Dip 169*f*
　Horizontal Cable Press 170
　Incline Bench Press 167, 168*f*
　Push-Up 169
chiropractic 49
coaches' roles 4-6, 41
communication skills 6
concentration 8
conditioning development
　about 177
　Cardio Machine Drills 185
　Full Gassers (212s) 183
　Half Gassers 180
　Hill Running 185
　110s 181
　Play Drives 178-180, 178*t*, 179*t*
　Power Training (PTs) 182*f*
　Stadium Stair Running 184-185
　Suicide Gassers 180
　Tempo Runs 183-184, 183*f*, 184*f*
　350s 180-181
　300-Yard Shuttle 181
confidence 8
consistency 5
coordination 89
core development 135-137

D

data collection 15, 16*f*
dynamic movement drills
　Back Bear Crawl 57
　Crab Walk 58
　Fast Side Shuffle 56-57
　Front Bear Crawl 57
　Inchworm 58*f*
　Lateral Walking Lunge 56*f*
　Reverse Walking Lunge 55*f*
　Slow Side Shuffle 57
　Spiderman 59*f*
　Tapioca 56

F
FASTER plan 50
fat 43
flexibility development
  about 64
  flushing 67
  postworkout stretching 64-65
  static stretching 64
  static stretching drills 65-67
  yoga and Pilates 67
foam rollers 49, 62-63
forearms development
  Rice Bucket 175
  Sledgehammer 176
  Wrist Roller 175
functional movement screening 10

G
general physical preparedness 10
gluteus development. *See* posterior chain
    development
goal-oriented training 4

H
Hammer Jammer machine 118-120, 119*f*
hamstring development. *See* posterior chain
    development
Hang Clean testing 12
hydration 46-47
hydrotherapy 48

I
In Pursuit of Excellence (Orlick) 6
in-season workouts
  about 237
  postseason training 243
  postseason training programs tables 243-
    246
  preseason training 237-239, 238*t*
  red-shirt players 242
  travel squad training programs tables 239-
    242
  travel squad training tempo 239

L
lower back development. *See* posterior chain
    development
lower body development
  Leg Extension 145*f*
  Overhead Stair Walk 150
  Pistol Squat 149*f*
  Plate Push 150
  Split Squat 149*f*
  Step Up 147-148, 148*f*
  Walking Lunge 146-147, 146*f*

M
machine-based power exercises
  Jammer Extension 118-120, 119*f*
  Push/Pull Circuit 120
massage, sports 48-49
massage sticks 49
mat drills
  Four-Point Directional Wave 94
  Four-Point Seat Roll 94
  High Knees 93*f*
  Mirror 94
  Quarter Eagle 95*f*
  Spinning Wheel 94
  Two-Point Seat Roll 93
  Two-Point Shuffle Wave 93
  Two-Point Sprint Wave 94
max effort work (1RM) 13
meals and meal planning 42, 46-47
mental conditioning 7-8
mental focus 45-46
mobility development 138-139
multilevel system of training 9-14

N
neck development
  Four-Way Neck 170, 170*f*, 171*f*
  Neck Isolation 173
  Six-Way Neck with Manual Resistance 171,
    172*f*
NFL Combine 13
nutrition
  about 41-42
  carbohydrate 42, 45-46, 47
  FASTER plan 50
  fat 43
  and hydration 46-47
  and mental focus 45-46
  protein 42-43
  recovery 47-49
  supplements 45
  top foods for performance 43-45

O
off-season workouts 218-236. *See also* spring
    workouts; summer workouts
  autoregulatory progressive resistance
    exercise (APRE) 191-192, 191*t*, 192*t*
  developmental training 189-190
  multilevel progression 190
  supplemental exercises 210, 211*t*
  training programs tables 192-210
  training tempo 190
Olympic lifting 11, 112
Olympic Lifts
  Hang Clean 113-114, 113*f*, 114*f*

Olympic Lifts, *continued*
    Hang Shrug 115-116, 115*f*, 116*f*
    High Pull 116-117, 117*f*
    Power Shrug 118

P
physical therapy 49
Pilates 67
player profiles 16*f*, 17, 19*f*
players
    personal development 5-6
    PR paradigm 8-9, 9*f*, 21, 39
    responsibilities of 6
plyometric drills
    Altitude Drop 108
    Balance Drills 104
    Box Jump 106
    Broad Jump 104-105, 105*f*
    Calf Shock Drop 108
    Depth Drop 108-109
    Diagonal Broad Jump 106
    Lateral Box Jump 106-107
    Medicine Ball Chest Pass 111-112
    Overhead Throwdown 112
    Plyometric Push-Up 110-111
    Slide Board 110
    Split Jump 110
    Squat Jump 109*f*
    Tuck Jump 107*f*
plyometrics 103-112
    lower-body 104-110
    upper-body 110-112
positive thinking 7
posterior chain development
    Glute Ham Raise 154*f*
    Good Morning 153*f*
    Hyperextension 152
    Leg Curl 153
    Reverse Hyperextension 152*f*
    Romanian Dead Lift 150-151, 151*f*
power development
    exercises 134
    lower-body plyometrics 104-110
    machine-based power exercises 118-120
    Olympic lifting 112-118
    plyometrics 103-104
    upper-body plyometrics 110-112
power lifts
    Back Squat 122-124, 123*f*
    Bench Press 131-132, 131*f*
    Board Bench Press 132-133
    Box Squat 124-125
    Dead Lift 129-130, 130*f*
    Extended Squat 128, 129*f*
    Floor Press 133

Front Squat 126-127, 127*f*
    Strongman 134
program philosophy and objectives 6-7
protein 42-43
PR paradigm 8-9, 9*f*, 21, 39

Q
quickness development. *See* agility develop-
    ment

R
Reaction, Acceleration, Change of Direction,
    Effort (RACE) drills 99*f*-100*f*
rotator cuff development
    Bridge Series 143, 144*f*
    Cable External Rotation 139-140, 140*f*
    Cable Internal Rotation 140-141, 140*f*
    Cuban Press 141*f*
    Full Can 141
    Scap Circuit 142-143

S
self-talk, positive 7-8
shoulders development 161-167
    Band Pull-Apart 166
    Face Pull 166-167
    Shoulder Circuit 162-165, 163*f*, 164*f*, 165*f*
    Shoulder Combo 166
    Standing Shoulder Press 161-162, 161*f*, 162*f*
    Three-Way Raise 166
    Two-Way Raise 166
skinfold method (body composition) 25-26,
    26*f*
sleep 48
speed development
    about 69, 88
    drills 71-81
    high- and low-intensity runs 82
    speed drills 82-84, 86-87
    speed groups 84
    speed improvement vocabulary 70-71
    summer training 84-85
speed drills
    Backward Run 77
    B-March/B-Skip 73
    Bounding 78
    Build-Up 84
    C-Skip 77
    Dead Leg 76
    Downhill Run 82-83
    Fast Leg 76
    Form Run or Stride 79
    40-Yard Stance and Start 80-81
    High Knee 74*f*
    A March/A-Skip 72-73

Partner Resistance 87*f*
Running Butt Kick 75*f*
Scramble-Up 79
Seated Arm Action 71
Single-Leg Hop 78
Sled Pull 86*f*
speed station 91
Stadium Stair Run 83
Standing Arm Action 72
Uphill Run 83
spring workouts
    about 213
    training programs tables 214-217
    training tempo 214
static stretching drills
    Butterfly 65
    Hip Flexor 66
    Lying Quad 66-67
    Seated Trunk Twist 66
    Squat Stretch 66
    Standing Hamstring 67
stationary dynamic movement drills
    Arm Circles 59
    Iliotibial (IT) Band 60
    Knee Tuck 60
    Knee Up and Across 60
    Trunk Rolls 59
strength continuum 9*f*
strength development
    about 121
    back 155-161
    biceps 173
    bodybuilding 134-135
    chest 167-170
    core 135-137
    forearms 175-176
    lower body 145-150
    mobility 138-139
    neck 170-173
    posterior chain 150-154
    power lifts 121-134
    rotator cuff 139-144
    shoulders 161-167
    stability 139
    triceps 174-175
    upper body 155-161
summer workouts
    about 217
    multilevel progression 217
    order of activities 218*t*
    training programs tables 218-236
    training tempo 218
supplements 45

T
team records 16*f*
Tendo unit 12, 13
testing and evaluation
    about 15
    anaerobic conditioning 38, 38*f*, 39*t*
    anthropomorphic measures 24-25
    checklist for 16*f*
    clubs 21*t*
    explosive strength 27-28
    functional movement screening 39
    goal sheets 17, 18*f*
    hip and groin flexibility 34-35, 34*f*, 35*f*
    horizontal explosiveness 30*f*
    lateral speed and agility 36-37, 36*f*, 37*f*
    lower-body strength 31-32
    male body composition 25-26, 26*f*
    off-season 22-24, 23*f*
    player profiles 16*f*, 17, 19*f*
    records 22
    schedules for 22, 40*t*
    standards 17, 20*f*
    straight-ahead speed 35-36
    upper-body endurance 32-33
    upper-body strength 31
    vertical explosiveness 28-29, 29*f*
triceps development 174-175
    Tate Press 174*f*
    Triceps Extension 175
    Triceps Pushdown 175

U
upper body development 155-161

W
warm-up
    about 53-54
    foam rollers 62-63
    in-season 63
    off-season 63
    postworkout flexibility 62
    pre-workout routine 61-62
warm-up drills
    dynamic movement drills 55-59
    sample routines 60-61
    stationary dynamic movement drills
        59-60

Y
yoga 67

About the Authors

Pat Ivey has been the associate athletic director for athletic performance at the University of Missouri since 2011, after serving the previous seven years as the school's assistant athletic director for athletic performance and director of strength and conditioning. During his tenure at Missouri, he has helped produce multiple first-round draft picks. He was also the director of strength and conditioning at the University of Tulsa from 2002 to 2004, where he directed the efforts of all 18 sport programs.

Ivey lettered as a defensive end for the Missouri football team from 1993 to 1995 and was named the strongest athlete in the program's history in 1995. He was signed by the San Diego Chargers after college and spent two seasons with the team. He also went on to play with the Denver Broncos and Green Bay Packers.

Josh Stoner has been the director of strength and conditioning at the University of Missouri since 2007, after serving the previous three years as associate director. Under his guidance, the program has produced five first-round NFL draft picks in three years (2009, 2010, and 2011). In addition to being responsible for the athletic development of the football team, he oversees the efforts of Missouri's remaining sport programs.

As the assistant director of strength and conditioning at the University of Tulsa from 2002 to 2004, Stoner assisted with the football player development program. He was also responsible for the women's basketball, men's soccer, men's tennis, women's tennis, track and field, and cross country teams.

For more from Pat Ivey and Josh Stoner, please scan this tag (or visit www.tinyurl.com/Ivey-Stoner).